GIUSEPPE RAMA

KU-545-628

A PRACTICAL GUIDE TO THE DISCOVERY OF

VERONA

HISTORY, CULTURE, FOLKLORE
AND CUISINE IN THE CITY OF LOVE

Edizioni LA LIBRERIA di DEMETRA

Editing, graphics and layout: Laura Turati
Photography: Arc-en-ciel
Sketches: Fabio Lovati
Translation: Marijke van Leuven

Special Thanks to Vanna Tridi for her valuable assistance.

In planning these itineraries the author has borne in mind the problems of the traffic and the road system and, therefore, where possible, has marked out a route which is best undertaken on foot.

To Romeo and Juliet

GUIDA PRATICA PER SCOPRIRE VERONA
Storia, cultura, folklore e cucina nella città dell'amore
1ª edizione luglio 1995
© DEMETRA S.r.l.
Via del Lavoro, 52 - Loc. Ferlina
37012 Bussolengo (VR)
Tel. 045/6767222 - Fax 045/6767205

Summary

Tradition

*markets, gastronomy, trade
fair, tourist attractions*

History

environment, natural attractions

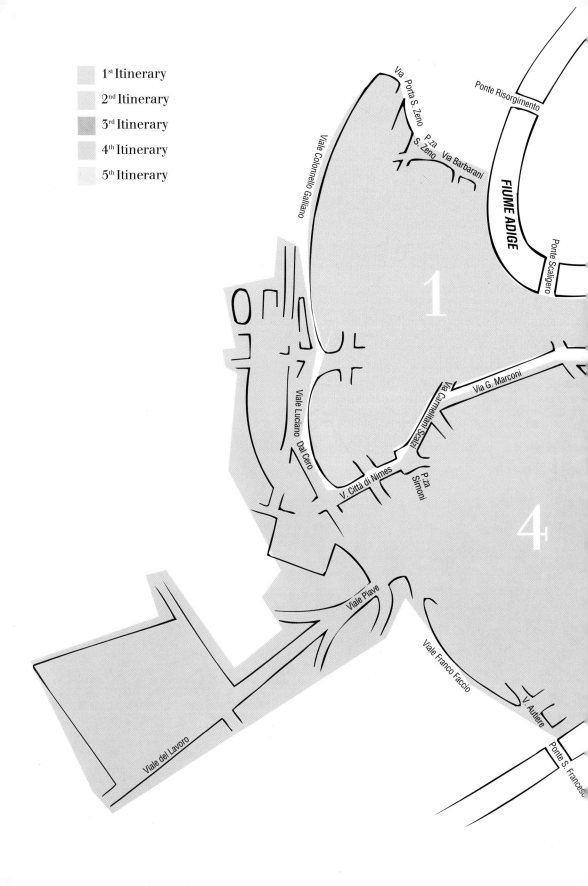

INTRODUCTION

Thanks to an important past, Verona's ancient monuments, picturesque squares and noble palaces give witness to a first-class cultural and artistic reality. The Arena (with its opera performances), Romeo and Juliet and the mythological places of their tragic love story, the volume of artefacts from the Roman and Medieval epochs and later the Middle Ages, the great number of churches and the silver ribbon of the Adige river render Verona a stimulating place to visit. The urban configuration, at times narrow lanes and at others the opening up of unexpectedly wide panoramas, not to mention its favourable geographic location at the end of the plains and the beginning of the Pre-Alps makes Verona a region full of variety and a natural bridge between Northern and Southern Europe. Its relative proximity to Lake Garda's eastern shores means, too, that foreign tourists enjoying a relaxing holiday inevitably finish up by paying a visit to the main city of the Adige Valley at all times of the year. With five itineraries we shall explore the most significant aspects of the city alternating historical attractions with those which are recreational, social and folkloristic. We shall punctuate a homogeneous, topographical route with a variety of anecdotes and titbits of information which will satisfy those who appreciate fine monuments, the enthusiastic dilettante and gourmet alike. A map found at the beginning of each itinerary highlights the salient points and where the subject merits in-depth treatment, this is given in the coloured boxes inserted in the main text.

GEOGRAPHY AND ECONOMY IN BRIEF

Situated 59 metres above sea level, Verona with its 265,000 inhabitants occupies the extreme western strip of the Veneto region. It borders onto four provinces: Trento to the north, Vicenza to the east, Mantova to the south and Brescia to the west and at its extreme south-east point it is wedged between the provinces of Padua and Rovigo for a short distance. Its fortunate geographic position at the end of the plains and the foot of the Pre-Alps is further heightened by the presence of the Adige river (the second largest river in Italy) which meanders through the city, thereby dividing it in two.

Even though the first settlements were up on the hill near St. Peter's Castle, the river was always important as a means of transport for goods especially from Trentino. Until last century a kaleidoscope of humanity was employed along the banks of the Adige: working the watermills, water-scooping machines, unloading wood and all kinds of goods. The disastrous floods of

1882 marked the end of these settlements and altered the geography of these quarters, especially that of Veronetta, irreparably. The economy of the city was badly affected, too, having briefly recovered from the period of Austrian domination. Rather than through the development of industry, however, Verona's rebirth has been due to its ability to insert itself into the world of international trade and agriculture, the latter renewed and continually up-dated by the fact that the city hosts one of the most important agricultural fairs in Europe. Trade, favoured by Verona's position as a key railway and highway junction (the north-south and east-west axes intersect here) will, in fact, continue to develop and be the backbone of the city's economy. But tourism, too, has an importance not to be underestimated, helped by the continuous extension of activity at the nearby international airport.

Verona, with its historic and artistic patrimony , its summer opera season in the Arena, combined with its proximity to Venice, Lake Garda and the Dolomites attracts thousands of visitors annually.

A BRIEF HISTORY

The city's origins are ancient, going back to an early nucleus of inhabitants on St. Peter's hill in a period which cannot be well defined. They lived near a ford which allowed them to connect with the plains and at the same time favoured rapid withdrawal towards the Pre-Alps when necessary.

Verona was subjected to various political influences: the Veneti, Euganei, Rhaetians, and then Etruscans, Gauls and Romans. It appears certain that in 3 B.C. the city was inhabited by the Veneti, a tribal people who, for years, maintained strong links with Rome, to the point where they even went to help her during the Carthaginan invasion of 225 B.C. This alliance favoured the expansion of trade and necessitated the opening up of new routes, as witnessed by the creation of the Postumia route in 148 B.C. A further testimony of loyalty to Rome was the offer of troops from Verona when the Cimbri invaded in 101 B.C.

After 89 B.C. (during the rule of Pompey) Verona became transformed into a flourishing Roman colony. At this time two bridges were constructed to link the city with the other side of the Adige: the Postumia and the Pietra. The following century saw the beginning of a golden age for Verona and the construction of the forum, capitol, amphitheatre, theatre, thermal baths, various temples and public works and a strengthening of the city's fortifications. St. Peter's Castle stopped being just an urban settlement and became a celebrated monument while trade received further impetus with the opening up of three important road networks. As well as the Postumia Road which connected Liguria with Illyria, the Gallica connected Turin with Aquileia, the Claudia Augusta (which began at Modena) passed through Verona to Germany and the Vicum Veronensium connected Verona with Ostiglia.

This state of well-being finished with the invasion of the Barbarians who had control of the city for centuries. Around 450 Attila arrived but was, fortunately, blocked by Pope Leo I near the Mincio river, while in 549 Theodoric, King of the Ostrogoths established his court at St. Peter's Castle. After a brief period of Byzantine domination it was the turn of the Lombards under Alboino (568). The Lombards, in fact, initially elected Verona as the capital of their kingdom.

In 774 Charlemagne conquered the city and his son, Pepin, championed projects of restoration and decoration with the help of Archdeacon Pacifico. In 888 Berengar of Tour, then King of Italy, established himself here and after him Verona was

The Ostrogothic king Theodoric came to a tragic end for he was mysteriously assassinated. The crime gave rise to legendary interpretations, one of which can be seen and read in two panels carved on the facade of the Basilica of Saint Zeno. Tradition holds that, after the fall of the Roman Empire, Theodoric became the new prince of Verona, that he had a splendid palace built on St. Peter's hill and there he lived a life of luxury and debauchery. One day when he was out hunting in a wood he saw an incredibly beautiful deer appear before him. Its powerful muscles, elegant form and the supple agility with which it moved, aroused the instinct of predator within the cavalier. He had never come across such game, to let it get away would be tantamount to a defeat!

He then embarked on a mad chase of woods, clearings, mountains and plains up and down the peninsula but the superb animal continued to remain in front and he sufficiently behind to prevent him from shooting the mortal arrow. Anyone else would have given in to the fatigue but not the proud Theodoric who, after infinite exertion, managed to confine the animal to the impervious slopes of the island of Stromboli. He was certain now that the extraordinary prey would fall into his hands: the sea and the smoke from the volcano would preclude any chance of escape.

Without a moment's hesitation, however, the beast defiantly faced the mouth of the volcano, descended the steep slope and went close to the boiling lava. Scornful of the danger, Theodoric imitated the deer but as soon as he flung his horse head-first into the chasm, the earth opened up under him and swallowed him up. So, the legend concludes, the devil disguised as a deer, dragged his servant into hell.

subjected to German imperial rule "when Otto I, King of Saxony intervened in the hope of calming the situation of anarchy which had developed as a result of the break-up of the Carolingian Empire. He became King of the Lombards in 951 and eleven years later founded the Holy Roman Empire".

Finally, in 1100 Verona became an independent city governed by consuls: in the bloody, internal power struggle which followed, an astute Ezzelino da Romano managed to have himself elected Governor and Captain of the people in 1226 and ten years later, Imperial Chancellor. When he died in 1259, he was succeeded by Martino della Scala (hence the adjective "scaliger"), the head of an important Veronese family which was to rule the city until 1387. The Scaligers were succeeded by the Visconti family (from Milan) and briefly afterwards, by the Carraresi. In 1405 the city surrendered itself, willingly, to the Venetians who ruled here (with a brief interruption of eight years) until 1797. This proved to be an epoch of peace and prosperity, brusquely ended by the arrival of Napoleon's troops.

After Bonaparte ceded the region to the Austrians with the Peace Treaty of Campoformio, the Treaty of Luneville (1801) decreed the division of Verona: right of the Adige to the Cisalpine Republic and left of the Adige to the Austrians. With the successive Treaty of Presburg (1806) the whole city together with the Veneto became part of the Kingdom of Italy but for eight years only, since in 1814 the Austrians returned once more. In reality this occupation was not too onerous and the Emperor considered the Veronese to be faithful citizens of the Austrian Empire. Aware of the city's strategic importance, however, the Austrians kept a constant eye on it for it was the main stronghold of the Quadruple Alliance. In reuniting Verona with the Kingdom of Italy in 1866, the long road towards national unity had been achieved.

VERONESE CUISINE

The Veronese cuisine is full of tradition, substance and imagination. The province's geography encompasses a wide variety of environments and this has had a positive influence on the gastronomy. The hilly area renowned for its wines, contrasts with the vast plain abundant in fruit and cereals. The waters of Lake Garda are home to a much-appreciated fish colony: a rare breed of carp and good salmon trout. Then, Lessinia's butter and cheese, Verona's famous "pandoro" (literally, golden bread) and Cologna Veneta's nougat are just a few more examples of local food. Within the province then, one is able to put together a complete meal and delicately dress it with local olive oil which is produced in the area between Valtramigna and Garda. Among the cereals, the rice grown in this province is considered to be one of the best in the world (Asia included!) both for its quality and capacity to remain intact while cooking. As for the fruit, let us mention the peaches grown in Pescantina, Villafranca, Bussolengo and Sommacampagna; the cherries of Val D'Alpone and Tramigna; the apples of Zevio and Belfiore; the chestnuts of San Giovanni Ilarione and the strawberries grown underground: a new technique in which Verona is leading Italy and Europe. The snails of Sant'Andrea di Selva di Progno are also worth a try.

As for the wine, we shall limit ourselves to naming a few reds: Valpolicella, Bardolino and Valdadige; and whites: Soave, Custoza, Durello, a little Lugano and Valdadige. The most representative dishes are gnocchi (a "pasta" made from potato); tagliatelle (pasta) with chicken livers; risotto with salted, minced pork and herbs; horsemeat stew and boiled beef served with a special local sauce (la pearà). Minor specialties include salame seasoned with garlic, a kind of sausage cooked in the embers and served with green cabbage, fried celery and to top off the meal, a good-sized piece of pandoro washed down with a glass of Recioto Valpolicella or Soave wine. There are many other dishes but often their origins lie in neighbouring provinces and hence it would be incorrect to quote them here.

The cuisine around Lake Garda deserves a special mention. Based, as to be expected, on fish it has managed to retain its own identity, fiercely independent of the city. We must note the anchovies and sardines prepared both on the grill with a little salt added or fried in oil with salt, lemon and a sage leaf. Anchovies can also be dried and later used as a condiment. Small trout are served with lemon and salt while the bigger ones are either grilled or boiled in water and white wine, and dressed simply with olive oil and lemon. Grilled carp is eaten the same way while pike is generally served with a little oil, parsley, carrot, celery, rosemary, sage, thyme and oregano. Small fish have a full succulent taste when fried but the eel, however, is always destined for the grill.

INFORMATION

Opening times of museums and main monuments

ARENA
Open each day from 8 a.m. to 6.30 p.m. During the opera season it is only open from 8 a.m. to 1.30 p.m. Closed on Mondays.

CATHEDRAL LIBRARY AND ART GALLERY-MUSEUM
Open Monday to Saturday from 9.30 a.m. to 12.30 p.m., except Thursday. On Tuesday and Friday it is open in the afternoon from 4-6 p.m. Closed in July.

CIVIC LIBRARY
Open Monday to Friday from 8.30 a.m. to 6.30 p.m. On Saturdays and during the month of August open from 8.30 a.m. to 1.30 p.m. Closed on Saturdays and feast days.

JULIET'S HOUSE
Open every day from 8 a.m. to 7 p.m. Closed on Mondays.

MONUMENTAL CEMETERY
Summer times: mornings 8.30-12.00; afternoons 2.30-6.30 p.m.
Winter times: mornings 8.30-12.00; afternoons 2.30-5.30 p.m. Open every day.

MINISCALCHI - ERIZZO FOUNDATION
Private visits: Monday to Saturday 4-7 p.m. On Saturdays, morning: 10.30 a.m. - 12.30 - afternoon: 4-7 p.m.
Guided visits: by arrangement, tel. 045/8032584. Closed on Mondays.

GALLERY OF MODERN ART "ACHILLE FORTI"
Open every day 8 a.m. - 6.30 p.m. Closed on Mondays.

GARDENS OF GIUSTI PALACE
Open in summer 8.30 a.m. - 8 p.m. During the other seasons the gates close at sunset.

AFRICAN MUSEUM OF THE COMBONIAN MISSIONARIES
Open Monday to Saturday 9 a.m. - 12.00 and then 3 p.m. - 6 p.m. On Sundays and feast days open from 3 p.m. - 6 p.m. Closed on Fridays.

ARCHAEOLOGICAL MUSEUM AT THE ROMAN THEATRE
Open from 8 a.m. - 1.30 p.m. Closed on Mondays.

CAVALSELLE FRESCO MUSEUM
Open from Tuesday to Sunday from 8 a.m. - 6.45 p.m. Closed on Mondays.

CIVIC ART MUSEUM
Open each day from 8 a.m. - 6.30 p.m. Closed on Mondays.

NATURAL HISTORY MUSEUM
Open each day from 8 a.m. - 7 p.m. Closed on Fridays

MAFFEI EPIGRAPHIC MUSEUM
Open each day from 8 a.m. - 1.30 p.m. Closed on Mondays

LAMBERTI TOWER
Open from 8 a.m. - 6.30 p.m. During the winter the tower is open from 8 a.m. - 2 p.m. Closed on Mondays.

Small markets in Verona

On Tuesdays: at Piazza Isolo, San Zeno, San Massimo, Borgo Venezia, Saval.
On Wednesdays: at Porta Vescovo, Borgo Trento, Ponte Crencano.
On Thursdays: Santa Lucia, Golosine, San Michele, Parona.
On Fridays: at San Zeno, Porta Vescovo, Volto San Luca, Saval.
On Saturdays: at the Stadium.
Third Saturday of each month: crafts exhibition, art and antiques in Piazza San Zeno.

Useful telephone numbers

Green Cross Ambulance	8001111
White Cross Ambulance	8033700
Verona Emergency Ambulance	582222/582118
Doctor on-call Sundays, feastdays and nights	913222/8072599
Carabinieri	112-597111
Finance Police/Customs Officers	8004025
State Police	113-8090611
Fire Service	115
Local Police	8078411
Road Assistance ACI	116
City Transport Authority (bus)	521200
Provincial Transport Authority (bus)	8004125
Railway Station Verona Porta Nuova	590444
Airport "V. Catullo"	8095666
Radio Taxi	532666
Information office Arena	590109/590726
Trade Fair Verona	8298111
Youth hostel	590360

NOTE: the telephone prefix for Verona is 045.

Porta S. Zeno

Ponte Risorgimento

FIUME ADIGE

Via Tomaso da Vico

Via Porta S. Zeno

Circonvallazione P. Maroncelli

P.za S. Zeno

Via Barbarani

V. S. Giuseppe

V. Scarsellini

Regaste S. Zeno

Via A. Rosmini

Via A. Lenotti

Str.ne A. Provolo

Vicolo San Bernardino

V. Picasano

Via A. Setti

Stradone porta Palio

Circonvallazione A. Oriani

Via Città di Nîmes

Via Carmelitani Scalzi

P.za Simoni

Via G. Marconi

V. Roma

Ponte Scaligero

Ponte Vittoria

V. A. Diaz

V. Oberdan

Corso Cavour

V. C. Cattaneo

FROM THE GATE OF SAINT ZENO TO CORSO CAVOUR

Porta (gate) San Zeno
- St. Zeno's Basilica and Abbey
- St. Proloco's Church - Regaste St. Zeno
- Church of St. Zeno in the Oratory
- St. Bernardino's Church - Palio Gate
- Zoological Gardens - Castelvecchio (Old Castle)
- Gavi Arch - St. Lawrence's Church
- Church of the Holy Apostles
- Church of Sts. Teuteria and Tosca
- Corso Cavour

A varied itinerary, rich in artistic moments and the panoramas offered along the footpath of the Regaste: one can enjoy the expansive Adige river, its majestic Scaliger bridge and surrounding hills at one and the same time. The route is dominated by the figure of Saint Zeno, Verona's bishop in 4 C and patron saint, after whom the basilica is named. The basilica is one of the most brilliant examples of Romanesque architecture as is the small, evocative church of St. Zeno in the Oratory near the river. Most of this itinerary takes place in the suburb of St. Zeno, a quarter which has always remained popular and which is the fulcrum of Verona's Carnival.

The route starts at ST. ZENO'S GATE (1541), actual headquarters of Verona's Carnival. Built by Sanmicheli, it is a minor work in comparison to the monumental PALIO GATE but it is appreciated for its compact structure and excellent state of preservation and the facade facing inwards is characterized by a portal decorated with coats-of-arms and plates. The SPANISH BASTION adjoins it - a noteworthy example of a military fortification, projected by the same architect. After passing through the gate one enters the suburb of St. Zeno. This is the liveliest quarter of the city where it is possible to grasp the true spirit of the Veronese. The visitor is pleasantly surprised at the number of pubs and eating places concentrated into a space of little more than a hundred metres and it is difficult not to enter into the festive spirit which filters out of the old osterias and modernized bars which are always full.

A large śquare, in need of reorganisation, hosts the BASILICA OF ST. ZENO MAJOR with its adjacent abbey bell-tower and the small Church of St. Procolo.

The Basilica of St. Zeno Major, of exceptional artistic, human and historical importance, occupies a special place in the hearts of the Veronese. A first, small church was built on the site between 372 and 380 A.D. to host the mortal remains and honour the memory of the African saint. Enlarged during the reign of Theodoric, it underwent various modifications over the centuries until the 12 C

St. Zeno's Gate, work of Sanmicheli.

It is impossible to outline all the eating places in the quarter of St. Zeno.

All are worth visiting and one can enter for just a snack or for a complete meal. Lovers of the city's folklore have spoken at length about the osterie (pubs) in St. Zeno, and this is certainly not the time or place to summarise them.

One cannot not mention, though, the most celebrated such as the trattoria "Al Calmiere" - at the controlled price - whose kitchen prepares typical Veronese dishes including the boiled meats served with the special pearà sauce; the restaurant "Antico Tripoli", a well-known hotel in the Orti di Spagna - Spanish gardens - quarter; the renowned pub "Alla Busa" - at the den - which has seen the daily vicissitudes of life for centuries and is the place to go for a taste of Veronese wines; the newish and most welcoming pub "Abazia" an ancient building which has been beautifully restored and offers a wide selection of snacks, in line with the tradition.

A word, too, must be given to the pub "Al Boscarello" - to the forester - which opens out onto a blind branch of the Regaste. Here, the people still love to honour the Marian fresco which faces the pub, in September - a harking back to the times when the lane filled up with chairs, the boatmen and grain merchants sat and smoked while brunettes spun wool and exchanged glances with the young lads who came by. Even here legend steps in, for it was claimed that Martino I della Scala (Governor of Verona) who was assassinated near the arch which links Piazza Erbe (the market square) with Piazza dei Signori, was in fact returning home from an armorous meeting at "Al Boscarello" then a grove (the pub came later) which extended down to the fronds of the Adige.

The Basilica of St. Zeno flanked by the bell tower (on the right) and the abbey tower (on the left).

when it took on its present shape. The pure Romanesque style of the facade in tufa with marble finishing touches at the top adorns Brioloto's magnificent rose window, commonly known as the Wheel of Fortune because the six carved figures represent various phases of the human condition. There is a gabled arch supported by two lions in red marble under the rose window (work of Nicolò Giolfino); in the lunette one can see St. Zeno stamping on the devil and almost at the bottom, a few bas-reliefs narrate the best known of the saint's miracles while further along the shelves of the gabled arch, the symbols of the months are carved.
The sides of the portal host a

The rose window by Brioloto adorns the facade of the Basilica of St. Zeno.

sequence of marble panels. Those on the right, attributed to Nicolò Giolfino are based on the theme of the Creation of Man and the Earth with the exception of the last two which depict Theodoric on horseback and the deer. Those on the left are by Guglielmo and narrate episodes in the life of Christ, except for the two lower ones which illustrate a duel between cavaliers and a duel between infantymen.
The PORTAL, with its famous bronze panels, is undoubtely the jewel of the facade. The 48 plates, whose origin is still under discussion, were definitely engraved by more than one artist and date back to the end of the 11 C or beginning of the 12 C. Both the wings repeat subjects already depicted in the marble panels but in more detail and with the addition of the miracles of St. Zeno. The BELL-TOWER rises up on the side. Slender and tall, it houses the oldest bells in Verona, cast by Gislimerio in 1149. In the middle of the grass one can see the entrance to a Roman tomb which is wrongly believed to be that of king Pepin, the Short-father of Charlemagne.
The CLOISTERS and brick ABBEY TOWER (with merlons on top) and adjacent buildings form one complex with the Basilica. This is all that remains of what was once a great and powerful Benedictine abbey. The cloisters, with elegant twin-columned arches and the picturesque niche which juts out into lawn, are lined with a number of monumental tombs. A small door takes one into what was once St. Benedict's chapel, nowadays used as a chapel for Mass in winter.
On entering the Basilica one is struck by its austerity. There are three aisles divided by weighty columns but the edifice continues

Above: the famous bronze plates which decorate the wings of the portal of the Basilica of St. Zeno.

To the left: the cloisters of the old Benedictine abbey which adjoin the Basilica.

on beyond the two red marble staircases to the upper church, while a central flight of steps leads down to the crypt where the body of St. Zeno is preserved. The walls are covered with fragments of frescoes, as various in style as in theme. Almost all are of unknown authorship but particularly important are some done by an unknown artist who worked between the 13 C and 14 C. By the main entrance, on the left, one cannot help but notice the large PORPHYRITIC CUP which came from a Roman bath, while tradition claims that it was given to St. Zeno by King Gallieno who

The statue of St. Zeno which is conserved inside the Basilica and nicknamed "St. Zeno laughing" by the Veronese.

had had it transported here by the devil. On the opposite side one sees Brioloto's baptismal font and Guariento's large stational Cross (14 C) hangs on the wall behind. Two wings of frescoes lead one to the upper church where, above the sacristy door, Altichiero's "Crucifixion" is to be admired, while to the side in an alcove sits the rather primitive 13 C statue of unknown authorship affectionately called by the Veronese "St. Zeno laughing", showing the saint smiling, with a fish suspended from his crook. The celebrated triptych (1457-1459) above the high altar, by Andrea Mantegna, commands one's attention. Taken away by Napoleon, it was later returned but minus the lower panels which were subsequently substituted by reproductions by Paolino Caliari (Veronese). The statues of the twelve Apostles surrounding Christ, the Redeemer which rest on the modern baluster, are probably the work of the Alemannic school and date back to the first half of the 12 C.

The 10 C CRYPT is made up of nine small aisles supported by forty-nine columns with Roman capitals and Romanesque decorations. Here lie the relics of St. Zeno, in a silver and crystal urn placed on a monolithic altar. As elsewhere in the basilica, there is a wealth of frescoes.

THE ABBEY TOWER is also adorned with frescoes but without doubt its masterpiece is the "Fresco of the Procession" which is placed at the second floor level along the external north wall of the tower, nowadays part of the abbey complex. Painted at the end of the 12 C and beginning of the 13 C, this gigantic work depicts a lively procession of people going to pay homage to a sovereign seated on a throne.

An important saint and a monument have been the protagonists of significant historical episodes, often remembered by the people in the form of legends.

Zeno was an African saint, probably born around 300 A.D. in Cesarea, Mauritania and consecrated Bishop of Verona on 8 December, 362 A.D. Even though he had fair skin he has continued to be represented in traditional icons as a dark-skinned man. (Take, for example, the famous statue located in the apsidiole on the left of the high altar.) This factor apart, Verona's patron saint enjoyed notoriety among the common people. This was due, in part, to the bronze plates on the portal of the church and, in part, to the records kept by the notary, Coronato and by St. Gregory, the Great, which were subsequently taken up and embellished by enterprising Zenonian Hagiographers. A religious recollection with disquieting undertones exists, however, and it links two factors constant to the history of Verona: the devil and the Adige.

We learn from St. Gregory, the Great that in the early period after Zeno's death, it so happened that in 589 the Adige was in flood and even reached the doors of the little church (the site on which the basilica now stands) thereby threatening the lives of the faithful gathered there. The river continued to rise vortically and the people, fearing they would drown, cried out in terror. At the invocation of Zeno a miracle occurred: the waters, as if moved by their own vitality, rose up to protect the temple and its devotees. Furthermore, the people were able to draw water to quench their thirst!

Another story recounts that, one day, Zeno was sitting on a boulder, fishing undisturbed when suddenly an ox crashed through a hedge and pushed the ploughman into the river, into a whirlpool generated by a capricious demon.

To the left: the apse of the Basilica od St. Zeno with Andrea Mantegna's celebrated triptych above the high altar.

Below: the crypt where the relics of St. Zeno are conserved in a silver and crystal urn.

The saint, however, was not ruffled. He made a sign of the cross and cried, "Away with you, Satan". Do not lead to death this man whom God has created".

The demon infuriated by this show of strength, retaliated by stirring up the waters even more. He then disappeared, but not before shouting defiance at Zeno, "If here I cannot gain souls, I shall go and seek them out in far-off places!".

The demon kept his word and within a few months Bishop Zeno was asked to intervene, for the daughter of King Gallieno was "possessed". The messengers who had called for Zeno secretly abused his generosity for while Zeno was getting ready to leave, they decided they wanted to eat. The stolen fish, however would not cook: it continued to jump around in the boiling oil, more alive than ever.

Exasperated, the devil meditated revenge. He challenged Zeno to a mighty match of "tamburello" in the big square in Verona. When Satan, whose turn it was to be beaten, hurled himself up from the Borago valley above Avesa (a village near Verona) he was so big that Zeno needed all the space of the Arena to drive him back. Zeno's face, however, continued to remain composed and there was a knowing smile painted on his lips. The struggle continued with no hits spared until one violent kick back from Bishop Zeno displaced an enormous mass of stone which trapped Satan in a cave from which he could only escape by using his horns and nails!

Once again the devil had lost and he had to pay the price: transporting an enormous tub of red granite from Rome to Verona in the time of a breath. It proved to be such a difficult undertaking that with the tension he left his fingerprints on the edge of the tub which can still be admired. For the devil dropped that immense petal of rock - by the main entrance (inside) to the basilica of the saint!

St. Procolo's Church faces into the same square as the Basilica of St. Zeno.

Just past the bell-tower stands another church, albeit small - that of ST. PROCOLO. Built in the 5 C it was named after Procolo, the fourth bishop of Verona and it served as a parish church until 1806. Its facade has a finely-built arch and fragments of 13 C frescoes.

Over the centuries it has undergone numerous modifications, the biggest projects being the intervention promoted by Archdeacon Pacifico in the 9 C and the most recent, this century, which have restored the edifice to its ancient dignity after the occupation by the French troops at the beginning of the 19 C reduced it, first to a theatre and then to a warehouse.

Of great interest are the tombs recovered from under the floor of the church and the restored frescoes in the crypt, some of which are extremely old. The

On the northern side of St. Procolo's church one can see the sepulcre of Tommaso da Vico: a 15 C nobleman who, by leaving a conspicuous bequest, was the legendary creator of Verona's Carnival - a beneficent event - one of the oldest in Italy and characterised by the "Papà del gnoco" (the father of gnocchi, a "pasta" made from potatoes). In former times, people who were less well-off were given quintals of gnocchi at Carnival. The enormous stone slabs which served as tables for the dispensing of the gnocchi can still be seen behind the fence of the grassy area which connects the southern side of the basilica with the northern side of St. Procolo's.

Five centuries of history, then, honour a dish which is both robust and delicate at the same time. A perfect amalgamation of flour and the soft paste of potato, the Veronese gnocco gets its form from the grater on which the mixture passes in order to polish it before adding a tasty sauce. A light covering of cheese adds the final touch to a dish which the great Veronese poet Berto Barbarani paid tribute to in:

> *And you, grater, work*
> *to give your gnocchi the miracle*
> *of speech;*
> *rendering pimply*
> *their surfaces*
> *so that the sauce will stick better.*

Tommaso da Vico's tomb outside Saint Procolo's Church.

columns and capitals in the crypt, all different in form and style, testify to a glorious past. Restoration projects have highlighted the strong link between St. Procolo's and the Basilica. There is, in fact, a continuity of artistic thought which allows one to predict that when the grand project of restoration is finally completed, a priceless artistic-historic patrimony will come to the surface.

After leaving St. Procolo's down the side street, one enters the lively Corrubio Square and then proceeds into via Berto Barbarani (a no-entry street for cars which must use the parallel street, via San Giuseppe) and straight down to the river, Regaste San Zeno - a tree-lined raised promenade which follows the right bank of the Adige. Looking north one sees the Veronese Pre-Alps while in the distance the pinkish marble caves of Mount Pastrello appear below the Mount Baldo. Opposite is what was once a vast horticultural area but has, since World War II, become a residential zone. One's view is framed by three large arches with merlons, the arches of the Castelvecchio Bridge - an anticipation of the majestic Scaliger construction.

But before going into the details of this important monument, let us deviate into Stradone San Provolo to visit the small Church of St. Zeno in the Oratory, the Monastery and Church of St. Bernardino and, a little further on, the Palio Gate.

The Church of St. Zeno in the Oratory (San Zeneto, in Veronese dialect) is reached by deviating to the right off the Regaste. It is the last Zenonian monument on our route and tradition has it that St. Zeno came to this his spot to pray. A first building in this honour dating back to the 8 C was destroyed by the flooding of the Adige. The actual edifice was realised in the 13 C. On walking through a courtyard one arrives at the entrance which has a Gothic door - all that remains of the

The Church of St. Zeno in the Oratory as seen from the front.

church of St. Anthony (which was about two kilometres away) destroyed by fire in 1827. Two statues of saints by Francesco Zoppi decorate the door.

The facade, sombre and well-proportioned is warmed by the colour of the brick and a geometric rose window embellished by pieces of perforation. The interior is graced by three aisles and one can admire a "Cruxifixion", probably the work of Domenico Brusasorzi. The side altars: the Bassani Chapel of 1482, St. Joseph's chapel of 1692 and another built in 1701 lead one past multi-coloured marble and statues to the main altar which is rendered human by the benevolent smile of the saint and protector.

In a corner on the right there is a large sandstone boulder supported by a Roman pillar on which, a Latin inscription informs us, Zeno used to sit to fish.

A fine, small, 14 C, semicircular gabled arch overhangs a secondary entrance while a Roman consul's seat set into an irregular wall is visible.

A small cloister of Lilliputian proportions (humble and graceful) adjoins one side of the church.

Back on Stradone (literally, large road) San Provolo one proceeds to the Monastery and Church of St. Bernardino. Protected by high walls, it has retained its ancient Franciscan appearance and serenity. The basic construction work was carried out about 1451 (the church was consecrated two years later) but we know that by 1466 the edifice had still not been completely finished.

The Gothic facade has a Lombard Renaissance portal. The three statues over the arch represent Sts. Bonaventure, Bernardino and Anthony. The bell-tower, too is made of brick, typical of all

Veronese churches of the epoch. An external colonnade has a lunette which shows episodes in the life of St. Anthony of Padova. The interior is centred on a main aisle which has an extremely high ceiling with wooden trusses. To the right, a side aisle (added on later) has many chapels. Of interest are: an artistic Renaissance holy water font at the entrance; the chapel of St. Francis (at the beginning of the side aisle) and frescoes of moments in the life of the saint by Nicolò Giolfino. In the panel showing the young Francis handing over his clothes to his father, one can see, in the background, a view of Verona with the Adige, the stone bridge (ponte della pietra) and St. Peter's Castle. On the altar there is a copy of an altarpiece by Cavazzola of

The austere facade of the Church of St. Bernardino which adjoins the convent of the same name.

the "Madonna glorified, with Sts. Anthony and Francis".

The Banda chapel is embellished by Bonsignori's "Madonna on the throne with Child".

The Medici chapel is an artistic jewel. Entirely frescoed by Domenico Morone and with statues of Sts. Anthony of Padua, Francis and Bernardino it has, however, suffered the insults of time and damp:

The Chapel of the Cross (or the Avanzi Chapel) is at the end of the aisle. It is adorned with paintings of the greatest artists of the Veronese Renaissance: Cavazzola, Giolfino, Badile and Francesco Morone. The latter's "Crucifixion" is worthy of note.

A lower chapel goes off to the right and is called the Pietà (Mercy). Enclosed behind a grill are a group of six statues in tufa, important for their expressive quality. Following on, by the presbytery is the luminous and special Pellegrini Chapel - fruit of Michele Sanmicheli's genius.

The central aisle, Gothic in style, is brightened by two long windows and a rose window on the facade and another rose window by the high altar.

The high altar hosts Benaglio's tryptych, a good copy of the celebrated work of Andrea Mantegna which adorns the altar of St. Zeno's Basilica. On the left, the 14 C pulpit and organ deserve a mention. The pulpit is said to be the most beautiful of its kind in Verona, with its elegant canopy on which the Rossi coat-of -arms stands out while the organ, unique in form and colour is further adorned by Domenico Morone's paintings on the two doors which enclose the keyboard and a console: depictions of St. Francis with the Stigmata and St. Bernardino holding the monogram of Christ.

St. Bernardino is always depicted with this monogram of three letters in Gothic script J.H.S. (Jesus

The picturesque cloisters of the Monastery of St. Bernardino.

Left: "Five holy friars" - one of the precious frescos conserved in the Morone Room, the ancient library of the Monastery of St. Bernardino.

"Christus Salvator" enclosed in a circle of rays. The saint loved this symbol and exalted the people to take it away and use it to invoke divine help in the name of Jesus. Cloisters surround the church and monastery, two are fully frescoed with episodes in the lives of Sts. Francis and Bernardino.

Finally, one should visit the old library called the "Morone Room". Its realisation was due to the initiative of a nobleman Lionello Sagramoso and it was frescoed by Domenico Morone but highlighted by his painting of the "Virgin on the throne and Saints" on the back wall.

Below: the external facade of the majestic Palio Gate by Sanmicheli.

Walking away from the centre but continuing along the same road one arrives at CORSO PORTA PALIO, a big road which is dominated by Sanmicheli's masterpiece, the grand Palio Gate. Originally called St. Sesto's Gate, this majestic monument has a facade with five arches each enclosed by two columns facing inwards to the city. The entablature is decorated with metopes and triglyphs while the walls are of ashlar work. The facade facing outwards is equally scenographic with three openings which are scanned by Doric columns and an enclosed loggia. The ZOOLOGICAL GARDENS are just beyond this gate.

Balestra's "Annunciation" conserved in the Church of St. Teresa of the Barefoot (S. Teresa degli Scalzi).

Returning inwards towards Castelvecchio one passes the large military hospital on the right. It was built by the Austrians between 1852 and 1854. Then one arrives at a church, ST. TERESA DEGLI SCALZI (OF THE BAREFOOT). Built between 1666 and 1750 (of octagonal design) by Pozzi, it is decorated with statues by Zoppi and Muttoni and altars by Puttini (one of which hosts a special "Annunciation" by Balestra. What was once the adjoining convent was later handed over to the military judicial authorities and it was here that Galeazzo Ciano (Mussolini's son-in-law) was held, along with others, during the Trial of Verona (for Treason) in 1944. A little further on one cannot help but notice the majestic ORTI PALACE, built on a design by Luigi Trezza and rendered special by four gigantic caryatids by Zoppi and Sartori. To note, too, are two churches: the Romanesque "All Saints" (Ognissanti) and St. Catherine's (15 C). A small lane on the right leads one to the 19 C ADELAIDE RISTORI THEATRE, a place which was once protagonist in the history of Veronese theatre. Nowadays, sadly, it lies in ruin. CASTELVECCHIO (the old castle) is the enormous complex which rises up at the end of Corso Porta Palio. It was built in a hurry between 1354-1356 on the orders of Cangrande II della Scala after a failed coup against him, organised by Fregnano. Guglielmo Bevilacqua designed the structure in such a way that it could guarantee his master an escape route north in the event of further popular insurrections. Its function was two-fold: that of a palace and that of a fortress. As a result the palace was to be constructed beyond the city boundary wall, the fortress just inside, with a series of internal corridors to connect the two

nuclei. The construction was realized in the area then called St. Martin in Acquaro. In ancient times the site had hosted a small Roman fort on the road which led to the city and had also functioned as a link between the two banks of the river. The rocks of the fort were successively used to raise the little St. Martin's Church and also, in part, to reinforce the pylons of the then-called St. Zeno's Bridge. We know the date the Castle's foundation stone was laid (22 May, 1354) but we do not know either the date of construction or who the architects of the Scaliger Bridge (that which replaced the old St.

Above: a view of the facade of the Palio Gate facing internally.

To the left: the facade of the Arsenal which was built on the left bank of the Adige near the Scaliger Bridge.

Zeno's) were. Perhaps it was projected at the same time as the castle. We know, however, that it was possible to transit the bridge (reserved for the Scaligers) only after 1375 under the rule of Cansignorio. The architect is thought to have been either Giovanni da Ferrara or Jacopo da Gozzo. Constructed entirely in brick, the bridge has three arches (each different) with pylons topped with merlons similar to those of the tower. The central bay boasts a light radius of 48 metres or more, and altogether the structure can be considered a masterpiece of engineering of the Middle Ages. It was mined by the German troops during World War II but faithfully reconstructed in the 1950s. As for the "Arsenale" Alberto della Scala wanted to have an arsenal protected by variously angled towers near the Adige river, hence the construction. The courtyard enclosed a number of old buildings and the little church of St. Martin in Acquario. In 1370

Below: Entrance to the bridge - a suggestive choreography of shapes, light and shade - taken from inside the Castle.

To the left: a spectacular nocturnal panorama of Castelvecchio and the Scaliger Bridge.

Cansignorio began confiscating land situated just beyond the bridge on the left bank with the objective of transforming it into Castle gardens, while the construction of the fortress dates back to 1376 when the votive fresco of the "Virgin with Child and Saints" was probably painted.
This fort has been subjected to many political and constructional vicissitudes over the centuries. The Carraresi ruled briefly from 1402 to 1405 but had picturesque decorations added, while the Visconti domination highlighted military characteristics which were subsequently reinforced during the Venetian epoch. The long period of peace which the city enjoyed under the Serenissima rule (that is, that of the Venetian Empire) encouraged, in fact, a progressive negligence of the monument but there was a drastic shake-up when Napoleon's troops arrived in 1797. The French set about destroying the towers and in 1804 they even planned the

construction of barracks in the Neo-Classical style (an unfinished project). This new building, with adaptations, remained intact even during the Austrian occupation until, in 1870, the opening of the road from the Campagnola (nowadays Borgo Trento and the zone beyond) to the city, brought alterations. The present design dates back to the 1920s when part of the old castle stopped functioning as a barracks and was assigned the role of MUSEUM OF FIGURATIVE ARTS (transferring the collection from the adjoining Pompei Palace). Restoration work continued under the direction of the architect , Forlati between 1924 and 126.This intervention transformed, above all, the facade of the Napoleonic Wing which was decorated with fragments dating back to the Middle Ages, recovered and brought there from palaces which had been pulled down when the embankments of the Adige were constructed in 1890. The merlons were also cleaned up and set in place, likewise the decorations on the internal and external walls.

Nowadays Castelvecchio is the home of the Museum of Figurative Art, a project which has included some remodelling and necessitated stylistic changes. Thanks to the work of Professor Carlo Scarpa layers of modifications over the centuries have been peeled away thereby allowing the identification and precise dating of the various historical and architectural phases of the building. The result has been the realisation of a functional edifice whereby open spaces alternate with closed-in spaces and visitors can pass freely from one exhibition room to another enjoying the external panoramas at the same time.

Turning left out of Castelvecchio

Cangrande II was definitely disliked by the Veronese. Of suspect and recalcitrant character, during his brief reign (1351-1359), he did not hesitate to act despotically, so much so that he earned the nickname "canis rabidus" or enraged dog. A mediocre statesman, he longed (notwithstanding his incapacity) to recreate those great political alliances which had allowed the Scaligers under Cangrande I to be known as one of the most splendid and important courts in the north of Italy. In order to pursue this objective he married Elisabetta, daughter of Ludwig of Bavaria and then went even further to try to enlarge his circle of imperial friendship by giving his sister, Altaluna to Ludwig, Marquis of Brandenburg, in marriage.

At the beginning of 1354 during one of his periods of absence from the city, his half-brother Fregnano, spurred on by political interests and incited by Visconti and Gonzaga, organized a revolt to overthrow him. Fregnano spread the word that Cangrande was dead; then he convened an assembly with the council and the people and succeeded in having himself named as the guardian of the legitimate heirs, Cansignorio and Paolo Alboino.

On hearing of the insurrection, Cangrande moved immediately, gathering a small army in Vicenza. Near Campo Marzio in Verona he came face to face with the enemy and beat them soundly. Fregnano instantly fled, hoping to reach the border with the Serenissima (Venetian Republic) but drowned in the Adige.

As a memorial, Cangrande had a church built on the site of the battle and called it "Our lady of Victory". Then he castigated his people by imposing new duties and heavy taxes.

It was, in fact, fear of further insurrection which pushed the Scaliger prince to hurry the construction of Castelvecchio but this was not enough to save him, for death awaited one night in the vicinity of St. Euphemia's Church in hand of his brother, Cansignorio (who then became Lord of Verona). This happened on the 14 December, 1359 and Castelvecchio had been completed for only three years!

An internal courtyard of Castelvecchio protected by a boundary wall.

Here is a summary of the main works housed in the gallery. The ground floor (5 rooms) is almost exclusively reserved for Veronese sculpture.

ROOM I. Reliefs and epigraphs of the late Medieval and Romanesque periods. A ciborium figuring the "Handing over of the law" (Christ between Saints Peter and Paul) by the sculptor Peregrinus came from the Cathedral; the tomb of Sts. Sergio and Bacco (1179); two female caryatids; a male figure (perhaps the work of Brioloto). Valuable evidence of the late Medieval period is preserved in the small chapel: late Roman epoch glass, Lombard jewels, silver plates with relief work, Lombard treasures of Isola Rizza; silver plates with relief work, a cross-shaped disc and a small urn-reliquary from San Giovanni in Valle.

ROOM II. Houses sculpture in sandstone from the first half of the 14 C, attributed to Maestro di Sant'Anastasia.
"St. Catherine of Alessandria"; "St. Martha"; "St. Cecilia"; "St. John, the Baptist"; "St. Bartholomew"; a group: "St. Zeno, Madonna and child" in red Verona marble.

ROOM III. Collection of works from the14 C but smaller in size than those in the preceding room.
"St. Libera"; "Cruxifixion"; "Madonna on the throne with Child".

ROOM IV. More works by Maestro di Sant'Anastasia
"The Virgin Mary fainting";
"Crucifixion"; "St. Bartholomew".

ROOM V. Collection of sculpture, mainly 15 C.
"St. Martin"; "St. Peter" (by Bartolomeo Giolfino); six panels in bas-relief (Ananias, Aaron, Daniel, Abraham, Jacob, Amos); headstone of Dinarato Spinelli (1335).

ROOM VI. On leaving room V, one walks along a passage to the Romanesque door by Morbio, where in a room, one can admire the bell which came from the Gardello Tower and was made for Cansignorio della Scala by Maestro Jacopo. The date 25 July, 1370 is imprinted on it and it depicts St. Zeno, the fisherman in relief.

ROOM VII. Having passed through Morbio's door one arrives at the main tower (torre Maggiore) and the room which follows. A series of very old bells are kept here: that of Federico della Scala (1321); that of Pietro della Scala (1358); that of the Church of St. Mary, Mater Domini (Mother of God - 1385) and another dated 1488. Furthermore, one can observe a capital which depicts the Virgin with Saints, 15 C.

ROOM VIII. Accessible via a gangway on the first floor of the castle. On display here is the only figurative fresco discovered during the 1924 project of restoration: a "Madonna with Child and Saints".

ROOM IX. The small rooms leading off the main hall introduce the works of the Veronese during the Middle Ages: a "Madonna breast-feeding" and a "Crucifixion" (frescos pre-Giotto); "Madonna on the throne with Child" (school of Giotto); "Battle between two cavaliers" (fresco from one of the Scaliger palaces); "St. Bartholomew and St. Gregory" (14 C table in Tuscan style); a reliquary which preserves precious14 C jewels and was found in via Gaetano Trezza in 1938 (buckle of precious stones and pearls encrusted in a gold plate); sword found in 1921 in the tomb of Cangrande I della Scala, together with the remains of lining and a piece of valuable, 14 C velvet.

ROOM X Contains what remain of the original decoration of the castle. "Incoronation of the Virgin" - second half of the 14 C and of the same school as Altichiero, as are also the fragments of sinopite.

ROOM XI Display of some rare examples of 14 C Veronese table drawings: "Holy Trinity among Sts. Zeno, John the Baptist, Peter and Paul' by Turone di Maxio (1360); in the centre, "Incoronation of the Virgin"; altar frontals of "Madonna with Child and six saints"; Thirty Bible stories; a polyptych depicting "Madonna with Child on the Throne, surrounded by saints and gift-bringers"; a polyptych by Tommaso da Modena of a "Nun offering St. Anthony of Padova a reliquary with St. James nearby".

ROOM XII Reveals a vast decoration of geometric motifs dominated by a frieze.
Includes pictures from the first half of the 15 C. "Madonna of the Rosary" is an example of ornate Gothic, attributed to Stefano of Verona; "Madonna of the Quail" attributed to Pisanello"; "St. Jerome" by Jacopo Bellini; "Christ in the Tomb"; "Adoration of the Magi".

ROOM XIII Veronesi and Venetian paintings from the first half of the 16 C. "Death of Mary" by Michele Giambono; "The Crucifix" by Jacopo Bellini; Polyptich from Aquila by Giovanni Badile; Triptych of "Sts. Cecilia, Tiburzio and Valeriano" by Antonio Badile and also "Madonna with Child, women saints and four doctors of the Church". Between the two triptychs are two tables with paintings of "Sts. Firmanus and Rusticus"; a statue of "St. John, the Baptist with symbols of the Gospels' by Maestro di Sant'Anastasia; four statues which come from Scaliger tombs; "St. Catherine of Siena" by Giovanni Martino Spanzotti of Piedmont; four parts of a polyptich with "Sts. Augustine, Stephen, Thaddeus and Bartholomew" from the Tirolese school, end of the 15 C.

ROOM XIV This small room hosts masterpieces by foreigners. " Still life" by Joachin Beuckealer; "Interior of a house with kitchen" by Marten Van Cleef (1566); "Woman with flowers" by Peter Paul Rubens (1602); "Concert at table" by Ambrosius Benson; "Portrait of a man" by Willem Key (1566); "Crucifixion" from school of Luca de Leyda; "View of a Port" and "Waterfall" by Hans de Jade (1657); "Portrait of F.R. Kolb" by Konrad Faber von Kreutzrach.

ROOM XV On the second floor of the castle. Collection of Venetan masters exclusively and depicting mainly Madonna and Child.
"Madonna and Child" (C1470) by Giovanni Bellini; "Madonna and Child", the "Nativity" from Bellini's studio; "Madonna and Child with St. Jerome" by Giovanni Mansueti; "Christ in Benediction", attributed to Jacopo de' Barbari; "Crucifix with the bust of a Monk in prayer", attributed to Cristoforo da Lendinara; "Madonna with Child" by Alvise Vivarini; "Sts. Martha and Mary Magdalen" by Giovanni Agostino da Ledi; "Madonna and Child" by Pier Maria Pennacchi; "Stoning of Stephen" by Andrea Previtali; "Sts. Catherine and Veneranda" by Vittore Carpaccio; "Madonna and Child" by Bartolomeo Montagna.

ROOM XVI Collection almost entirely dedicated to Francesco Morone (C1471-1529), an artist who was fundamental to the Veronese school of painting at the end of 15C.
"Madonna with Child"; "Sts. Bartholomew and Francis"; "Sts. Sebastian and Paul"; "Sts. Anthony Abbot and Rocco"; "St. Bernard and a holy man"; "St. Clare and two holy women"; "The Stigmata of St. Francis"; the "Nativity and St. John, the Baptist"; altarpiece of the "Holy Trinity"; "Sts. Francis and Bernard" (tables) perhaps by Domenico Morone; "Sts. Bartholomew and Rocco" (painter uncertain).

ROOM XVII Dedicated almost entirely to the works of Francesco Bonsignori (C. 1460-1519), a Veronese painter who worked in Mantua alongside Andrea Mantegna above all, as a portrait painter.
An "Adoring Madonna with Child"

(1483); "Madonna with Child and Saints"; "Sts. Paul and George" by Giovanni Caroto; polychromatic statue in wood of "St. James" by Giovanni da Zebellara.

ROOM XVIII Displays almost entirely the works of Liberale da Verona (c. 1445-1529), a great miniaturist but also a valid fresco and table painter. "Triumph of Chastity and Triumph of Love" (front of a marriage chest); two "Nativity scenes with St. Jerome"; "Christ being taken down from the Cross"; "Madonna of the Goldfinch"; altarpiece with "Sts. Paul, Jerome and Francis"; "Madonna with Child" (also called Madonna with Jasmin" probably by Nicolò Giolfino; "Fall of St. Paul" by Bernardo Parentino.

ROOM XIX Works manifesting the Veronese Humanist movement at the end of the 15 C and beginning of the 16 C. Fragments of geometric frescoes are also preserved on the walls. Two frescoes with "St. Sebastian" and "Sts. Jerome, James and Lawrence"; altarpiece from the Miniscalchi Museum depicting the "Sacrifice of Isaac between two donors"; "Augustus and Sybil" by Gian Maria Falconetto; "Sts. Catherine, Leonard, Gottard and Dominic", and "Sts. Rocco, Anthony, Onofrio and Lucy" by Domenico Morone; Allegories of liberal arts and a predella showing stories of "St. Barbara" by Nicolò Giolfino.

ROOM XX Concentration of masterpieces from Veneto, second half of 15 C. "Madonna with Child" by Carlo Cirelli; "The Holy Family with a Saint", perhaps by Andrea Mantegna; "Madonna with a Fan" by Francesco Beraglio; "Madonna embraced by her child" by Domenico Morone; "Resurrection of Christ" by Jacopo da Valenza; " Madonna with Child and St. Margaret" by Francesco Bonsignori.

ROOM XXI Exposition of Lombard material collected on Veronese territory and dating back to the period

prior to the end of 7 C. About 300 artefacts, mainly weapons and jewellery.

ROOM XXII This is the room of the tower and fort where a series of 14 C daggers and objects from diverse epochs are displayed. On the wall is a portrait of Pase Guerienti in military uniform. Moving on one passes a step where a statue of "Cangrande on horseback" (c. 1335) is placed, artist unknown.

ROOM XXIII Houses almost exclusively the works of Paolo Morando (1486-1522), pupil of Francesco Morone and innovator of the, then fashionable, new style of Veronese painting.
Five big canvases with "Stories of Christ"; four tables with "Sts. Joseph, John the Baptist, Bonaventure and Bernard"; "St. Thomas in disbelief"; "Madonna with Child and St. John, the Younger"; altarpiece showing "Madonna with Child and Sts. Anthony and Francis surrounded by the seven Cardinal and Theological Virtues"; "Youth with picture of a puppet" by Francesco Caroto; "Young Benedictine Monk" by Francesco or Giovanni Caroto.

ROOM XXIV Prevalent here are the large altarpieces by Girolamo dai Libri (c. 1474-1555), painter and miniaturist.
"Nativity scene with rabbits"; "Madonna with Child and Sts. Peter and Andrew"; "Madonna with Child, St. Joseph, Archangel Raphael and little Tobias" (1530); "Pietà (Mercy) by Francesco Caroto; "Madonna with Child blessing the people and Sophonisba", also by F. Caroto; "Madonna with Child and Sts. Joseph, Jerome, Anthony Abbot and Rocco" by Francesco Morone; "Portrait" (presumed to be) of Girolamo Savonarola by Moretto.

ROOM XXV Collection of paintings which demonstrate the movement towards a Venetan school in the mid 16 C.

"Conversion of Saul" by Giulio Licinio; "Contest between the Muses and the Pierides" (front of a chest) by Jacopo Tintoretto, "Adoration of the Shepherds" by Jacopo Tintoretto; "Marco Pasqualigo" by Domenico Tintoretto. An entire wall of this room is dedicated to Paolo Caliari (called Paolo Veronese, 1528-1588): his altarpiece Bevilacqua-Lazise showing a "Madonna with Child and angels"; "Sts. Ludwig and John, the Baptist with their benefactors Giovanni Bevilacqua-Lazise and Lucrezia Malaspina"; "Christ being brought down from the Cross"; "Stories of Esther"; "Concert" by Giambattista Zelotti.

ROOM XXVI Draws together the last threads of Veronese Mannerist painting.
"Portrait of Antonio Bevilacqua" by Orlando Flacco; "Head of a Bishop" by Domenico Brusasorzi; "Christ shown to the people" (1562) and "Sts. Thaddeus and Francis of Paola" by Paolo Farinati; "Medea restores old Aeson to youth", perhaps by Orlando Flacco; "Plea for an end to the Plague in Venice" by Jacopo Palma, the Younger; "Portrait of a man", also attributed to Palma, the Younger; "Christ is flagellated" and "Adoration of the Magi" by Alessandro Turchi.

ROOM XXVII Early 17 C Veronesi paintings.
"An old man with glove", "An old man reading" (1626), "Saint Anthony reading", "Portrait of a monk and the doubting St. Thomas" by Marcantonio Bassetti (1586-1630); "Portrait of a young man" by Bernardo Strozzi; "Flagellation of Christ", "Madonna with Child and Sts. John, the younger and Francis", "Adoration of the Shepherds" by Alessandro Turchi; "Pietà with Mary Magdalen and two angels", "Pietà with angels", "Joseph with Putifar's wife" by Pasquale Ottino; "Christ appears before his mother after the resurrection" and "Liberation of St. Peter from Prison" both by Marcantonio Bassetti; "St. Rocco" by Paolo Veronese;

"Christ in the garden of Olives" (1616) and "St. John the Baptist preaching" (1617) by Gianbattista from Trentino; "Portrait of a young man", perhaps by Felice Brusasorzi; "Pietà with St. Francis in adoration" by Alessandro Turchi; a "Lady" by Dionisio Guerri; "Tobias and the angel" probably by Guerri; "Parable of the workers of the vine" by Francesco Maffei.

ROOM XXVIII Display of 17 C Venetan masterpieces.
"Crucifixion" by Giulio Carpioni; "Foundation of St. Mary Major" by Alessandro Turchi; "Christ and the adulteress" by Giovanni Antonio Galli; "Judith", "Flight into Egypt" and "Sts. Peter and Paul" by Pietro Ricchi; "Madonna with Child and Mary Magdalen in prayer" by Gian Benedetto Castiglione; "Jupiter sprinkles Semel with ashes" by Luca Ferrari.

ROOM XXIX Collection, first and foremost of 18 C Veronese and Venetian paintings.
"Self-portrait ", "Prophet Isaiah", "Death of Abel" by Antonio Balestra (1666-1740); "Bacchus and Arianna" and "Diana and Endymion" by Luca Giordano (1632-1705); "Eliodor makes Ono deliver the treasure from the temple" by Giambattista Tiepolo; Sts. Peter Orseolo, Theobald, Paris and the Blessed Lucy Stifonte" by Giandomenico Tiepolo; "Transfiguration of Christ" by Gianbettino Cignaroli; "Jupiter and Semel" perhaps by Odoardo Perini; "Annunciation" (1699) by Alessandro Marchesini; "Allegory of Fame crowned by merit" by Simone Brentana; "David horrified before Saul's weapons" by Sebastiano Ricci; "Adoration of the Shepherds" by Federico Bencovich; "Angel inspires Judith" by Gian Giuseppe Dal Sole; "Battles" by Antonio Calza; "Sketches" by Gianbattista Pittoni and GiandomenicoTiepolo; "Rebecca at the well" by Antonio Diziani; "Coffee" by Pietro Longhi; "Portrait of Alessandro Maffei" by Joseph Vivien.

Facing page: above, Arch of the Gavi which is next to Castelvecchio and of Roman origin.

Below, the imposing facade of the Canossa Palace.

one comes to a small square with the Roman ARCH OF THE GAVI which dates back to the first century A.D. although only situated here since 1932. It is a sepulchral monument and was designed by the architect Lucio Vitruvio Cervone in memory of his family. Originally it stood in front of the Clock Tower of Castelvecchio, at the intersection of via Postumia and the suburban road. It was moved in 1805 because it was blocking visibility; in fact, some differently-coloured stones on the footpath indicate still now where its original position was. Over the centuries many of the limestone blocks of the Arch have had to be replaced. It has four facades: two major and two minor, with Corinthian columns. At the top rests a sculpted figure of Medusa.

The small square opposite is called Pasque Veronesi (Veronese Easter Square) in memory of the insurrection which broke out over the 1797 Easter period: the general populace against the arrogance of Napoleon's occupational force. It was a bloody revolt and there were many martyrs.

CORSO CAVOUR begins at this point. It is important because it followed the course of the old Roman road, Postumia, and has always been a major arterial road, originally projected to facilitate the movement of urban traffic! In the 16C a number of famous palaces were built along here. On the left, immediately past the Gavi Arch, one sees the majestic CANOSSA PALACE built between 1530 and 1537 on Sanmicheli's design. The lower part of the building is in ashlar work and the palace is "crowned" with mythological statues. The ceiling of the main lounge was once decorated with Tiepolo's fresco of Hercules rising to the temple of Glory but,

unfortunately, the masterpiece disappeared when the building was bombed on 25 April, 1945. The adjacent MUSELLI (EX POMPEI) PALACE is the home of the Bank of Italy in Verona. Smaller than the previous palace, it is unusual for its three chimney-pots which are built as towers. Then follows the PORTALUPI PALACE at number 38, built between 1802-1804 on Gaetano Pinter's design.

After St. Lawrence's Church we come to the 15 C. MEDICI PALACE at number 10 and the Baroque Palace at the end of the road. The latter, built in 1665 on Prospero Schiavi's design, has a grand entrance with windows adorned with masks, shells and cornucopia, and 14 C mediallons are visible above the balcony. Inside there is a staircase of the same epoch and a Tuscan-style Madonna.

Almost hidden from view, just beyond the Portalupi Palace, stands the Romanesque church dedicated to ST. LAWRENCE. A Gothic portal surmounted by a statue of the saint leads one into a small courtyard which is full of archeological finds. The building constructed in alternating strata of tufa and stones testifies to a rich history. Its present form is ascribed to the 12 C but its origin lies in the 8 C. The facade is adorned with two Romanesque towers which have stairs that once led to the women's gallery, while on the south wall there is a side entrance with a Renaissance arcade. The bell-tower (15 C, but later rebuilt) is on the right of the apse.

Inside, the church has a nave and two aisles with five apses, and the cross-shaped pilasters alternate with columns. The side aisles have bohemian vaults - a form of reinforcement and "protection" from the porticoes of the women's gallery above.

The absence of adornment exalts the architecture.

Apart from a few 13 C. and 15 C.

Ownership of a palace in Corso Cavour was, for the nobleman, once a sign of prestige for it attracted important guests. A constant coming and going of society people fed the gossip and comments did not lack vanity and jealousy. Because of this, the Muselli (formerly Pompei) Palace, relatively modest in comparison to the majestic Canossa and Portalupi Palaces, suffered the satirical Latin epigram: "Inter Canem and Lupum ridiculus Mus" - between the dog (Canossa) and wolf (Portalupi) lies the ridiculous "mus" (elli) (in Veronese dialect, "musso" means "ass").

Instead, the parties held at the Bevilacqua Palace were legendary. It was there that Count Mario created the highly celebrated "abridged musical" in the 14 C. The nobleman decorated his palace magnificently and completed it by setting up a library and art gallery. He paid his musicians and artists well and supplied the former with old, precious instruments. Word of the abridged musical spread through the country and all celebrities who passed through Verona stayed at least one night to enjoy the music at the Bevilacqua Palace.

Facing page: above, the Carlotti Palace.

Below: the exterior of St. Lawrence's Church.

frescoes, the right apse of the presbytery houses a 15 C. "Ecce Homo" in carved wood, while on the high altar there is an altarpiece by Domenico Brusasorzi depicting the " Madonna glorified with Sts. Lawrence, John, the Baptist and Augustine". There are two elegant sarcophagi and Nogarola Valmarano's sepulchral seal (16 C.) are placed along the left wall. An interesting feature of both this church and that of the lower church of St. Firmanus is the singular plan; that is, the two small apses of the transept are situated on the wall facing east (instead of north or south) and this siting is typical of French churches of the epoch.

Now, let us take a look at the palaces on the right of Corso Cavour.

The BALLADORO PALACE with Trezza's facade and its classical style follows immediately after the Pasque Veronesi Square. The BEVILACQUA PALACE (c. 1534) of Sanmicheli's school is actually the state high school "Ippolito Pindemonte" (a technical Institute) these days. The ground floor has large, rectangular windows which are scanned by ashlar pilasters and adorned with the busts of

Roman warriors. The upper floor has a majestic balcony with balusters and Corinthian columns of various styles. Above the door arches there are sculptures of reclining figures, and a sculpted band with mouldings completes the ornamentation. Then there is a small square with the Church of the HOLY APOSTLES and its annex, the CHAPEL OF STS.

Above: the facade of the Bevilacqua Palace, embellished by an elegant balcony.

TEUTERIA AND TOSCA.
The SCANNAGATTI PALACE at number 11 is a glittering example of Veronese Renaissance architecture: its portal has been attributed to Domenico da Lugo. The edifice, probably the work of Gabriele Frisoni (1495-1505), has undergone various modifications and additions including the three statues by Spiazzi which depict the PAST, PRESENT AND FUTURE. It currently houses the botany and pre-history laboratories of the city's Natural History Museum.
The CARNESALI PALACE (first half of the 16 C.) is noteworthy for its elegant balconies. One passes the GIOLFINOS HOUSE - the family of celebrated painters and wood-carvers - in the wide curve which precedes the Borsari Gate. The facade still has a few picturesque and decorative

The Giolfinos' house which still has a few interesting frescoes on its facade.

fragments of frescoes, among them a "General on horseback" and "Duel between Cavaliers" by Nicolò Giolfino.
The CHURCH OF THE HOLY APOSTLES with its adjoining chapel dedicated to Sts. Teuteria and Tosca almost faces ST. LAWRENCE'S. Nowadays, it stands at the back of a tree-lined square, removed from the noise of the city traffic.
It is an old church: it already existed in the 8 C. However, various extras have been incorporated over the years: a funereal arch on the north side in the 15 C, two 19 C chapels, and apses stylistically extraneous to the Veronese school and thought to have been inspired by the French. The complex, including the bell-tower, is Romanesque in style and on the south side there is one wing of a cloister which was reconstructed in the 18 C.
The church has one central aisle with three apses which are framed by red marble Renaissance arches. A badly neglected fresco entitled "Christ with the Cross and St. Rocco" found in the small apse on the right is thought to be the work of Nicolò Giolfino. Also to be noted is the 14 C. stational Cross of the Giotto school above the first altar on the left, and the canvas with St. Augustine painted by Turchi (called Orbetto) on the internal wall of the facade.
The "chapel" dedicated to STS. TEUTERIA AND TOSCA is considered to be one of the oldest shrines of worship in the Veneto. Originally possibly a Roman sepulchre, it has undergone various transformations over the centuries but recent restoration has brought back some of its original glory. The edifice was at some point silted up and as a result its form of a Greek Cross became transformed into that of a

square and during the 16 C an opening in tufa along the north side was made. The oval windows which correspond in style to the two Bevilacqua tombs are, however, definitely 18 C.

Access to this chapel is through the sacristy of the Church of the Holy Apostles. The tomb of the two saints lies above the red marble altar, held up by four small columns which are supported by small square pilasters (1160). The sculptures on the arch depict the "Virgin with Child on the throne being venerated by Sts. Procolo, Teuteria and Tosca". The tomb of Francesco Bevilacqua, soldier and adviser to Cangrande II who died in 1368, is on the right of the altar while on the left of the arch one sees the coat-of-arms and, on the right, the family crest. There was a Pietà in the middle once but it is now walled in above the sepulchre. Opposite in three bays, are the tombs of Gianfrancesco, Antonio and Gregorio Bevilacqua, in which representations of the virtues of Faith, Hope and Charity have been sculpted.

The Baptismal font in the centre is supported by a pedestal of three dolphins intertwined (in Renaissance style) and a modern concha. But in a corner one can see the large 13 C. baptismal font which was carved out of a single slab of marble and in which, it is said, Blessed Maddalena di Canossa was baptised.

Interior of the Church of Sts. Teuteria and Tosca Above the altar the tomb of the saints is conserved.

The CHURCH OF THE HOLY APOSTLES, like that of SAINTS TEUTERIA AND TOSCA and also that of SAINT LAWRENCE sprang up along the Roman road which, on leaving the Forum followed the city boundary wall to the Gallieno Gate - later to become the Gate of the Borsari (Affairs) - and continued south towards the Arch of the Gavi.

A medieval legend recounts that Teuteria, daughter of the King of England, was deceived by Oswald and sought refuge in Verona at the home of Tosca, Bishop Procolo's sister. Tosca led a life of solitude inside a grotto whose opening was defended through divine ordinance by spiderwebs strong enough to serve as bars, and it was here that the two young women were protected from Oswald's interference.

Teuteria and Tosca lived together for the rest of their lives. Oswald repented and converted to Catholicism and later he, too, became a saint.

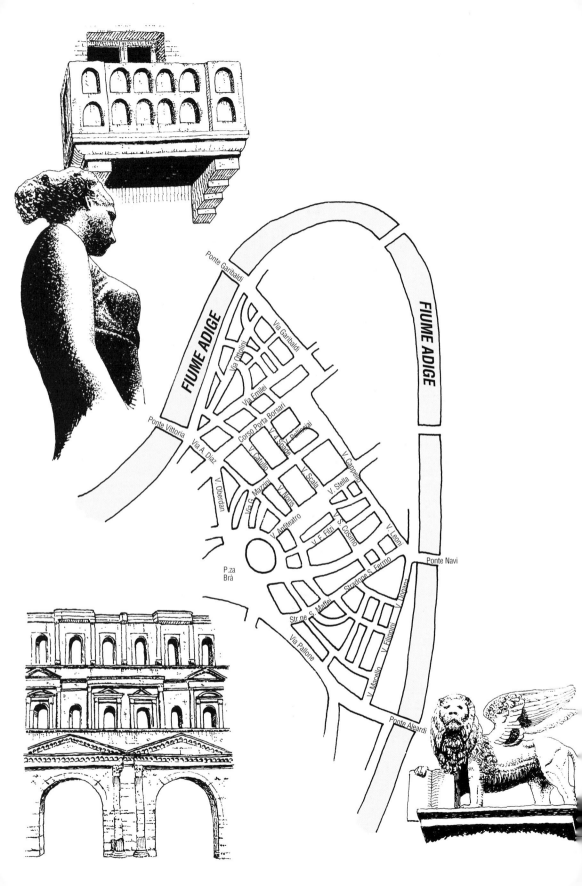

FIUME ADIGE

FIUME ADIGE

Ponte Garibaldi

Via Garibaldi

Via Ottolini

Via Emilei

Corso Porta Borsari

Ponte Vittoria

Via A. Diaz

V. T. Sarina

V. P. Pellesina

V. Catullo

V. Scala

V. Cappello

V. Stella

V. G. Mazzini

V. Noris

V. Oberdan

V. Anfiteatro

V. Cosmo

V. S. Cosmo

V. F. Filzi

V. Leoni

Ponte Navi

P.za
Brà

Stradone S. Fermo

V. Trogana

Str.ne S. Maffei

V. Filippini

Via Pallone

V. Macello

Ponte Aleardi

From the Borsari Gate to Mazzini Street via the Market Square (Piazza delle Erbe)

Porta (gate)dei Borsari - St. Euphemia's Church
- Church of St. John in the Forum - Miniscalchi
-Erizzo Museum - Piazza delle Erbe (Market Square)
- Juliet's House - Porta dei Leoni
- Church of San Fermo (St. Firmanus Major)
- St. Nicholas Church
- Church of St. Mary della Scala (of the Scaligers)
- via Mazzini

This itinerary is full of history and art. It is a continuation of the preceding one and takes in a large part of ancient Verona on the right banks of the Adige. The Market Square is the central point, the spiritual fulcrum which was once the Forum. The geometric Roman town-planning grid made up of decuman and pivot points radiated from here and it was in this area that the Medieval council buildings were first built and, later on, some of the most important Scaliger buildings.
So much history is, of course, not devoid of poetic and, perhaps, frivolous moments. Take, for example, Juliet's house and its famous balcony (mythical story of a forbidden love), and the promenades and shops of Mazzini and Cappello Streets, worldly aspects of undoubted attraction.

At the end of Corso Cavour, immediately before walking through the Borsari Gate (gate of business) one sees Via Armando Diaz on the left. By crossing the Victory Bridge - designed by Ettore Fagiuoli - one arrives at the modern, residential suburb of Borgo Trento.

The Roman, BORSARI GATE took on its name during the Medieval period for it was here that tax exactors collected the duties on merchandise on behalf of the bishop and canons. In the Roman epoch it was, in fact, known as Jove's Gate because there was a small temple dedicated to Jove nearby, lustrals of which remain scattered about in the gardens situated in front of the city's Monumental Cemetery.

Built in the first half of the first century A.D., the Gate was constructed on the maximum decuman through which the via Postumia ran. It was built in the white stone of the Valpantena (a valley near Verona) behind the pre-existing Republican Gate whose only trace today is the external facade which consists of two barrel-vaults 3.55 m. wide and 4.12 m. high flanked by two semi-columns fluted with Corinthian capitals. The "new" gate has a second storey with two flattened tympani which support a cornice on which six windows rest. The two external windows are embellished with a triple frame which is dominated by a triangular tympanum, while the two central ones (just as elegant) form a single unit thanks to the interweaving of twisted columns enclosed in a simple entablature. The second and fifth windows have a simply decorated profile. The third storey also has six windows in line with those below but they are more slender and crowned simply. On the inside it is possible to see a band of eight rows of brick which experts have identified as the point where the now-disappeared back part was attached. An inscription on the lower architraves testifies to the restoration of the walls under the orders of Gallieno in 265 A.D.

The Gate is 13 m. high and 12.93 m. wide. On its left is the 14 C SERENELLI PALACE whose basement includes parts of the Roman wall.

After passing through Borsari Gate, one proceeds along the street of the same name to the Forum. In the late Middle Ages running races were held along this stretch of road. Dante actually watched one of the competitions and duly cited it in a tercet of his "Divine Comedy". Important monuments are found along this street and its adjacent

Facade of the Borsari Gate, facing the exterior. This is all that remains of the Roman construction placed there with the intention of limiting the main decuman gate.

side street, rendering the zone one of the most interesting of the city. Looking upwards to the left one cannot help but notice ST. EUPHEMIA'S CHURCH a block away. Built in the early 1100s it was originally very small, but it was subsequently enlarged by the Augustine Friars when they took it over in 1262. During that century it underwent radical restoration and modification for, among other events, it was repeatedly damaged by military requisition and bombings.

The Neo-Gothic Italian-style facade has an elegant marble portal and two sepulchres: the one on the left, Baroque in style; that on the right, of the 12 C. There are another two urns on the left side of the building, near the small door which is dominated by a gabled arch.

The church has a single nave with a barrel-vaulted ceiling and the walls are scanned with side altars, most Baroque in style. The third side altar on the right hosts a "Madonna in Heaven and Saints" by Brusasorzi.

The sixth is dedicated to the

Traces of the ancient wall Gallieno had constructed are still visible in Farina (flour) Court.

In the time of Roman Republic, Verona was already a flourishing city enjoying an optimum position both militarily and commercially. This, however, called for an adequate system of defence - city walls with points of entry from the most important roads of communication: the Postumia which went from east to west and the Claudia Augusta from north to south. The first city wall, then, was erected. It was 12 metres high and made of bricks which were stuck together with a paste of sand, lime and water and reinforced at intervals with square-based towers. Proof of this wall's existence was provided when excavations carried out in via Leoncino (a small street behind the Arena) in 1967, brought to light part of it.

The Alemanic invasion (in 258 A.D.) forced the emperor, Galliano, to build a second wall seven years later: about 8 metres from the original, as testified by an inscription on the architrave of the Borsari Gate. Because of the urgencyof construction the wall was not intended to be a monument but rather, a strong and solid structure capable of defending the city, and the materials used reflected this: mainly rocks salvaged from necropoli found just outside the gates. The part of this wall which has remained most intact and includes even the Arena, is best seen in Mura Gallieno Square, via Diaz (Serenelli Palace) and then along the del Guasto Lane and the nearby Farina (flour) Court.

Madonna della Salute (of health) which it is popularly retained, contains a miraculous statue.

The seventh, Madonna of Perpetual Help hosts an altarpiece by Gianbettino Cignaroli. Twin chapels open up beside the presbytery: to the right the Spolverini Chapel houses some of the most significant artistic pieces in the church; to the left, the bell tower chapel is nowadays dedicated to St. Rita. The Spolverini Chapel still has flooring made up of tombstones while the latter appears to have undergone quite a lot of adaptation with valuable red marble slabs finishing up on the wall.

There is evidence of real artistic mishandling in the division of two frescoes, one placed on each side of the presbytery: Stefano da Verona's "Last Judgment" and "Madonna and Saints". At the back of the apse Dal Verme's marble mausoleum reminds one of the Scaliger tombs. Felice Brusasorzi's canvas "Our Lady of the Assumption, David and Moses" overhangs it.

To be noted along the left wall are: the wood-decorated organ, the

----

A shadowy event which took place centuries ago, had the Church of St. Euphemia as indirect protagonist. While moving tombstones in 1873, various skeletons even from the Middle Ages, came to light. The story goes that among these were also the remains of Messer Turco and Zenobia, wife of the renowned painter, Nicolò Giolfino, who had lived about one hundred metres from the church.

Giolfino, the betrayed spouse, on discovering his wife with her lover had, it seems, killed both in a fit of rage.

----

pulpit which is adorned with a painting by Ludovico Dorigny and the baptismal font in red Verona marble (1601).

Going back to Corso Porta Borsari, via Ostie Lane, we find ourselves in front of St. Matthew's Lane (vicolo San Matteo) which has a church of the same name. Documents of 1105 already mention it but we know it was deconsecrated in 1806 after having undergone various alterations. A little further on, set into the corner of a house, is a shelf dating back to the Roman epoch depicting "Triton sounding the bugle" and a "Head" by Gorgone. At number 44 one can admire the FATTORI PALACE followed by the REALDI PALACE at number 36 with its reliefs by Francesco Zoppi. Then one comes to a brick building with arched windows: a bas-relief above the portal depicts the "Trinity, Our Lady and archangels Michael and Raphael". The asexual appearance of the sculpture suggested the name for the ensign of the stalls which were once here, known as the Seats for the Elderly. Number 27 is a precious example of Scaliger Gothic architecture with its equilateral arched windows and tufa and brick construction.

The next side street is via Quattro Spade (four swords). Of note here is the ex-Dolci Palace (now a cinema), a 15 C Gothic house and a little further on, an old square tower of the late Middle Ages made of brick with a foundation of stone blocks. On the left along the Corso once again, one comes to the Romanesque , CHURCH OF ST. JOHN IN THE FORUM constructed in tufa, stones and brick.

This place of worship received its name from the nearby forum. The wall which lines the street is characterized by two large windows and a precious Renaissance portal in marble, dominated by three statues: Sts.

To the left: the brick facade of St. Euphemia's Church.

Below: St. Euphemia's Church has a single nave. Prevalently Baroque in character, the walls are lined with side chapels.

The Church of St. John in the Forum. Its name is due to its proximity to the ancient Roman Forum.

Domenico Brusasorzi. Certainly very old, this small church was rebuilt in 1172 after a fire. This fact is recorded in an epigraph preserved in a small 15 C tabernacle found on top of a sarcophagus with a 14 C base, but its interior has no specific features, however. Continuing along the same side one comes to the COURT OF THE SGARZERIE which is characterized by a loggia - both in need of repair. One enters through an arch and this is where the wool and cloth market instituted by Alberto della Scala was held, from 1299 to 1400. Opposite, between St. Mark's Lane and the adjacent blind alley, St. Mark's Well (pozzo), the TREVISANI-LONARDI home shows off frescoes of Roman ostentation and allegorical scenes by Giovanni Maria Falconetto. The CONTARINI PALACE which is almost adjacent, was probably built by Domenico Curtoni.

The house at number 7 was the birthplace of the novelist, Emilio Salgari (1863-1911), and on the left, the GARDELLO (or Clock) TOWER announces one's arrival at Piazza delle Erbe.

The Piazza delle Erbe was developed on the site of the ancient

John the Evangelist, Peter and John the Baptist. The lunette depicts a (neglected) fresco by Nicolò Giolfino: St. John, the Evangelist at Patmos, (Greece), while in an alcove one sees a "Christ being taken down from the Cross" by

At number 15 D, almost directly in front of a small church, one sees the entrance to a tiny bar called "CAFFE' TUBINO". The passerby cannot resist stopping in front of the window to admire the varied merchandise which awaits one on the other side of the threshold. This is not just any bar: the one and only room has standing space only and the three tiny, rickety tables are used for resting cups on. But one cannot help but remain amazed by the miraculous equilibrium obtained: behind and all around the bar the walls are lined with perfumed containers of every style and shape, a composite universe of sought-after blends of tea, coffee, orzo and chocolate-mixtures and impromptu inventions ready to be tasted by refined "experts" or simply by people who enjoy a good drink.

Customers from the other side of the Alps stop to enjoy an exceptional capuccino while even the most cold and collected Anglo-Saxons are amazed at finding an intimate corner among colonial descriptions of tea (yes, even in wild Italy!) but not having a teapot with them, finish by giving into a national weakness, that of buying little boxes of sweets decorated on the outside with cats, young girls or romantic landscapes.

Roman Forum, where, until the end of the 8 C one could still see the walled porticoes. This is undoubtedly the historic centre and the heart of the city. During the Middle Age the original vast rectangular space became transformed into an ellipse to create an area on which to build municipal buildings.

One, the Merchant's House (already then) demonstrated the Scaliger policy of making the square an economic-mercantile centre based, above all, on the wool trade.

Nowadays, the square houses stalls of all kinds and is also a relaxing place for a drink or snack. From an artistic point of view, it is able to offer a complete panorama of the inhabitants' vicissitudes over the centuries. The various colours and kinds of building materials used render this one of the most luminous and suggestive squares in Italy. Streets, lanes, other squares and arches radiate from here, giving the visitor an extensive choice of route.

Before describing the monuments in the centre of the square, we shall mention those situated on the perimeter of the square and in the adjoining streets. Coming from Corso Porta Borsari, the first imposing structure on the left is the GARDELLO TOWER with the merlons. Built in brick in 1370 by Cansignorio, it has a bell enclosure at the top made up of windows with two lights with Gothic arches and double columns in red marble. Because of its chiming clock (expressly wished by Cansignorio), the tower is known almost exclusively as the Clock Tower. The small lane beside it leads one to Monte Square, the ancient Roman Capitolium, where the Monte di Pietà constituted in 1490 still has its offices. Number 20 of the nearby via Emilei is worth noting: it is the 15 C WORM PALACE with its

To the left: the loggia of the Sgarzerie Court.

Below: an evocative aerial view of the Market Square (Piazza delle Erbe).

Above: the typical market stalls which crowd Piazza delle Erbe.

Gothic-Renaissance coat-of-arms. And not less striking is the old MINISCALCHI PALACE at number 2 Via San Mammaso with its Gothic portal which is highlighted by refined windows with twisted columns. Built in the second half of the 15 C and restored during the following century when its facade was frescoed by Michelangelo Aliprandi and Tullio India, the palace became the custodian of the Miniscalchi-Erizzo Foundation.

Inside, the rooms house antique furniture, archaeological finds, sculptures, bronzes, marbles, ivories, Renaissance armoury and 16 C and 17 C paintings. Returning to Piazza delle Erbe, immediately after the Gardello Tower, one sees the MAFFEI PALACE (1668), home of an old Veronese family and the illustrious man of letters, Scipione Maffei. This building, in late Baroque style, occupies the north side of the

Right: facade of the Miniscalchi Palace (home of the Verona Savings Bank).

square. The ground floor has five large ashlar doors while the first floor has five large windows with balusters and masks on the tympanum, articulated by Ionic semi columns. Above, the second floor has smaller windows which are separated by pilaster strips and plates engraved with family mottoes and achievements. The facade is completed with a baluster at the top, on which stand statues of Hercules, Jupiter, Venus, Mercury, Apollo and Minerva.

One moves on, then, to the east side of the square, the first part of which is occupied by the MAZZANTI HOUSES, what remained of the Scaliger DOMUS BLADORUM after Matteo Mazzanti's interventions in the first half of 16 C, while the Renaissance portal can be dated to 1840 when the spicery was destroyed by a fire. Fascinating is the facade with its marble mirrors (late 15 C) and giant frescoes of Ignorance, Prudence, Envy, Struggle between the Giants and Providence painted by the Mantuan, Alberto Cavalli (one of Giulio Romano's pupils) towards 1530. The back of these houses, reached from Corso St. Anastasia or, more suggestively through Barbero Alley, preserve important evidence of the Middle Ages highlighted by the Mazzanti staircase and painted decorations. Especially important is the Renaissance well curb with an architrave supported by two columns, known as the Mazzanti Well.

The DOMUS NOVA (House of the Judges) adjoins the Mazzanti Houses. It was built in the 18 C as an extension of the Municipal Chambers to which the DELLA COSTA ARCH is joined. This building was the home of judges and chief magistrates but over the centuries its original form has disappeared. The arch has the bone

of a cetacean suspended from it, thereby dating it about 16 C.

The REGIONAL PALACE is linked to the CARCERI TOWER. Its date of construction is uncertain but it is thought to be late 13 C. It not only looks out onto Piazza delle Erbe but also Piazza dei Signori (of the Gentlemen), the old market and via Cairoli. The tufa and brick facade underwent alterations in 1524 (Renaissance Style) and in the 17 C, a heavy, formal contortion.

At the back is the characteristic Romanesque courtyard called the OLD MARKET. In the 15 C. it was the grain market. Bordering onto a high colonnade with windows with three lights and open on three sides, this cloister conserves a few 14 C frescoes. The Gothic staircase of the Regional Palace (1446-52) which once led to

A detail of the Mazzanti Houses which still manage to conserve extensive fragments of frescoes on the facade.

the Court of Assizes, is worth noting. Inside, the CHAPEL OF THE NODARI (dialect form of "notaries") houses some beautiful masterpieces.

To the right: the staircase of the Regional Chambers with its fascinating Gothic lines.

Below: the slim lines of the Lamberti Tower, for centuries home of the resounding bells which have shaped the lives of the Veronese.

The LAMBERTI TOWER rises up out of this mass of palaces. 83metres high, it dominates the city. Begun in 1172 by the Lamberti family, it underwent a number of phases of construction and was only completed in 1464. Its bells, the work of del Rengo and della Marangona have shaped the lives of thousands of Veronese over time. The first bell was originally used to announce public meetings, the second served as a fire alarm. On the west side of the square a number of houses cum towers rise up - testimony of what was, until 1924, the Jewish ghetto. Then follows the DOMUS MERCATORUM (Merchants' House). Built in 1301 at the express wish of Alberto I as a place of trading (for wool), it was later subjected to various alterations, especially in 1600. Only since the end of the last century has an effort been made to restore it to its rightful dignity. On the corner one can see Girolamo Campagna's statue of the Madonna (1607). The small XIV NOVEMBER SQUARE follows. It is dominated by a statue by Egidio Girelli which records the massacre of 1915 when the Austrians bombed. Back on Piazza delle Erbe the row of Renaissance houses which follows were constructed on top of the Roman curia.

To be noted are the CRISTANI HOUSE at number 23 (which conserves frescoes by Girolamo dai Libri: "Madonna, Saints and Children" and "St. Peter is assigned the keys"), and the house at number 27 with its frieze of the "Incoronation of Mary" by Liberale da Verona.

The west corner of the square, directly opposite the Gardello Tower, is occupied by the CURIONI HOUSE (1575) which has a balcony decorated with military trophies. There is a capital or rostrum in the

To the left: the elegant structure crowned with merlons of the Domus Mercatorum.

centre of the square, better known as the "berlina", which was constructed on the orders of the governor, Galeazzo d'Este, in 13 C. The space was an important public meeting place; in fact, ceremonies of investiture of public office, band concerts, popular meetings and protests, all took place here, as did acts of public corporal punishment for cheats and blasphemers, such as beatings or immersion in the bath which is beside the rostrum. On the north side the marble column of St. Mark (1523) stands out: the winged lion and Venetian coat-of-arms testify the people's loyalty to Venice, following the period of Imperial rule under Emperor Maximilian I (1509-17). South of the column is the fountain with the statue of "Madonna Verona" which has a curious history. A Roman artefact, image of a goddess, it was taken from the Campidoglio and placed in the Forum in 380. Lost for a period, it was then refound but headless and partially destroyed. Put together again, crowned and adorned with the scroll ornament "Est iusti latrix urbs haec et laudis amatrix" (the city is the promoter of justice and lover of praise), Cansignorio had it placed above the fountain in 1368.

The ancient column which the condemned were tied to and left to endure public insults was near the berlina. This column, perhaps the work of Antonio da Mestre (1401) has been moved to the extreme south-east corner of the square and now supports a pyramid dais. On the south side of the square the central shopping streets, via Cappello and via Mazzini, begin. They form the traditional promenade for the Veronese and tourists alike. Two minutes' walk along via Cappello, however, will

Below: the ancient rostrum, called the "Berlina", conserved in Piazza delle Erbe.

To the discerning eater in search of something special, it would be a pity to miss this shady corner behind Piazza delle Erbe. In a lane arrived at by climbing one of the two short flights of steps which lead off via Pelicciai into a small square, and then turning left one sees, at 3 Corticella San Marco, a big lantern which marks the "12 APOSTLES" restaurant. The entrance could be mistaken for one of the exits off the small court, but a quick glance at the emblem on the door which indicates that this restaurant is a member of the chain "BUON RICORDO" (happy memories), reassures one that the location is exact.

The interior offers discreet rooms frescoed with Scaliger motifs while the tables laid with measured austerity let the contained refinement breathe, apt for those who are seeking a special place. The atmosphere of "suspect" familiarity turns into one of confidence when one meets Giorgio Gioco who encourages the guest to try a new experience which far outstrips the simple banality of a meal.

The history of the "12 Apostles" is ancient and its founding brings back to mind the story of the inquisitive women by Goldoni, both for its epoch and subject. Tradition has it that the lack of comfortable resting places was a serious problem for the merchants of the nearby square (piazza delle Erbe) who were forced to roam around in search of a quiet spot where they could spend an hour with a glass of wine in hand.

So, at the end of the 18 C., a group of twelve merchants chose the actual 3 Corticella San Marco as their retreat. The long table for the twelve foundation members quickly attracted comment and it was not long before this pub became known as the "Osteria of the 12 Apostles".Its fame spread quickly and already by the end of 19 C, the osteria was considered a place for discerning palates. During the course of this century, Gioco managed the restaurant for over 60 years.

One of the specialities is the cooking of food in a bread paste thereby giving it a particularly suggestive appearance especially the sturgeon: the "shell" adheres perfectly to the fish, outlining its form, while the porous quality of the pasta absorbs the fat therein aiding the digestion. This sophisticated culinary technique is Roman in origin. Later on, during the Middle Ages, the custom was to decorate the crust with fine gold leaves, giving the food an aspect of opulence.

D'Annunzio was a regular patron when in the city and it was on one of these occasions that the then manager, Antonio Gioco, asked the poet if, in his opinion, the food should be judged by the taste and size of the servings or by the way in which it was presented at table.

D'Annunzio did not know, but out of curiosity, decided to organize two banquets at the "Vittoriale". First, he assembled a group of well-known gourmets and had them served mediocre-quality food on fine porcelain with valuable cutlery and accompanied by an evocative atmosphere achieved by a delicate play of light. Then he called in the second group of friends whom he fed exquisite food served on cheap plates, lighting the tables and rooms with bright colours. The verdict: the mediocre food was judged to be optimum while the excellent food of poor quality. The appearance obviously counts! The poet furnished the chef with his findings and in return, received a number of bottles of excellent Soave wine.

This restaurant has won, among others, the Berti and Fogher awards and, opening up progressively to an intellectual high society clientele, it instituted the literary award "The Twelve Apostles" in 1969.

A charming foreshortening of a street which dates back to the Middle Ages, the lane where the "12 Apostles" is located.

family) is sculpted. Facing interally into the courtyard is the famous marble balcony (restored in 1935 by Antonio Arena) which played an important part in the story of the two unfortunate lovers. Below, Nereo Costantino's statue of the heroine stands forlornly nearby. The rooms of the house have been restored to the original plan.

The house was, in fact, auctioned in 1905 for 7,500 lire after suffering years of neglet which saw it used as a home for noisy carters and their muddy carts. On that occasion sympathetic Italians and foreigners - even well-known Parisians - put pressure on the City Council to buy the building.

After considerable debate the Council bought the old edifice on 8 July, 1905. The historical value of the house was attested to by the German poet, Heine, who in talking about palaces adjoining Piazza delle Erbe mentioned that "Near this square is a palace said to be that of the Capuletis since a hat as been sculpted above the main entrance. Not far from it is a church (San Francesco al Corso) whose chapel you are shown and where,

Juliet's house with its famous balcony.

Immortalised by painters including Bianca Dall'Oca, this column rises up from a pedestal with spirals at the corners and nowadays supports a shrine in whose niches we see the figures of the Blessed Virgin, Sts. Peter the Martyr, Zeno and Christopher (1929).
More than a century it was positioned near the central rostrum and was commissioned by Gian Galeazzo Visconti who had the symbol of his personal army carved on it.
After 1405, however, Verona was ruled by the Venetian Republic and, as was to be expected, all signs of the presence of the Viscontis were chiselled away. The column's attribute of antiquity is, therefore, relative but justified in respect to the "new" column erected at the other end of the square (piazza delle Erbe) to support the winged lion of St. Mark-symbol of the Venetian Republic.

lead one to JULIET'S HOUSE. The brick, 13 C house is adorned with merlons and is approached through an arch and covered walkway which leads into a small courtyard. At the top of the arch on the right a coat-of-arms of a hat (emblem of the noble Capuleti

An interior view of the Civic Library which also houses busts of Verona's illustrious citizens.

The legendary story of Romeo and Juliet took place in 1303 when the leader of the people was Bartholomew I della Scala. There are no existing documents which demonstrate with certainty the origins of the Scaligers (i.e. the della Scalas), a family which, for about forty years, managed to impose itself on other factions and successively to extend its own influence well beyond the city's confines. Their arrival did not succeed, completely, in appeasing the animosity of the quarrelling parties, even if Alberto I della Scala was highly praised for his efforts in that direction. The policy of reciprocal tolerance was also pursued by Bartholomew I who, at least, managed to assuage the parties involved in the brawls which now and then flared up on the streets of the city on the Adige.

Two families, in particular, nourished a sordid rancour: The Capulets (Capuleti or Cappelletti or Dal Cappello) who were Guelfs (papists) and the Montagues (Montecchi or Monticuli) who were Ghibellines (imperialists). Both were of illustrious descent: the Capulets were perhaps related to the counts of San Bonifacio and had merited a mention in one of Dante's celebrated tercets which underlines the climate of bloody rivalry that characterized the country at that time. The antique rivalries appeared to have calmed down when, in 1183, a marriage between members of rival factions was celebrated: a will-o'-the-wisp, in so far as the mother convinced her 15 year-old son to stab his Uncle Sauro, Count of San Bonifacio, in the back. Not surprisingly, fighting broke out again to the point whereby in 1206, the city was put to fire and sword and some of the houses of the Montagues were destroyed. The latter promptly organised revenge. The following year, in fact, the Counts of San Bonifacio were expelled from Verona but they re-entered with the help of the Mantuans and forced the Montagues to take refuge in Peschiera from where they returned only in 1213. In 1320 the Montagues were actually banished definitively from Verona for having plotted against Cangrande della Scala. They took permanent refuge in Udine. Let us not forget that Juliet was a Capulet and Romeo a Montague.

according to tradition, the unhappy couple were united".

One hundred meters further on, next to the bell-tower and remains of the ancient church dedicated to St. Sebastian, one sees the CIVIC LIBRARY whose foyer is lined with the busts of illustrious Veronese. Instituted in the 18 C., its shelves are filled with over half a million incunabulum, manuscripts and prints.

Continuing on, one arrives at the GATE DEI LEONI (of the lions), restructured and in its present form since 1959. The gate, which owes its name to a few ornamental figures found on a sarcophagus dug up in the vicinity, was built at the point of intersection between the final extremity of the Roman axis and the line of the Roman wall. During the Middle Ages it was known as St. Firmanus'Gate, due to its proximity to the church of that name (San Fermo) and in the 18 C. it was, in fact, called the Gate of the Judicial Forum. It is a twin construction, dates back to about the first century A.D. and is made up of an internal facade of the late Republican period and an external one of the Imperial period. They are about 60-90 cm. apart. The older construction, in brick and terracotta, was three storeys high, of which only one remains. The Imperial gate is more refined and was built in the white stone of Lessinia (the mountain range behind Verona). The barrel-vaults were adorned at the sides with two fluted semi-columns. An inscription on the architrave records the name Titus Flavius Norico. A triangular tympanum leads to the middle storey made up of three windows which have been well-preserved and above is half of the hexahedron with one twisted column and its Corinthian capital. Recent digs carried out there below the road surface, have brought to light one of the two towers which were positioned at either side of the external facade of the Republican Gate.

In the narrow lane beside the gate is the 14 C. VERITA' HOUSE which has a superb portal in 15 C. Ionic style, and on the inside grotesque paintings by Paolo Farinati.

The street finishes at the bridge called Ponte delle Navi (bridge of the ships), but before arriving there one cannot help but notice the elegant Gothic apsidal of the CHURCH OF ST. FIRMANUS MAJOR, the entrance of which is in the large street which winds round on the right.

ST. FIRMANUS MAJOR was built towards the 8 C. in memory of the martyrs, Firmanus and Rusticus.

What remains of the ancient Roman Lions' Gate.

Legend has it that, during the time of Christian persecution, the nobleman Firmanus and a relation, Rusticus were denounced to the Emperor. Notwithstanding the fact that they knew what the consequences would be, they refused to deny their faith in Christ. Taken to the big amphitheatre in Verona, they were hurled into the flames but came out miraculously unharmed.

In the 9 C. the Benedictines enlarged the church and later still, the Franciscans (when they came) organised other modifications which embellished the building: enriching it with spires, cusps and works of art to the point whereby it quickly became the most important church of the city. The Romanesque style is combined with Gothic: for example, the facade shows, in the centre at the top, a window with three lights flanked by two round windows while below, in the middle section, a window with four lights breaks up and lightens the tufa and brick-striped wall. The imposing Romanesque portal which is preceded by a deep splay made up of fine stone steps, and a frescoed lunette dates back to the 14 C. Aventino Fracastoro's arch is set into the side. (He was physician to the Scaligers in the 13 C.). The side entrance which is extremely ornate, is dominated by a domed portico. The apses are of importance: the side ones are Romanesque, while the central one is Gothic, decorated with cusps and pinnacles and illuminated by large, grand windows with Gothic arches.

The bell-tower is a unique construction. It looks like a big cone surrounded by four spires while elegant arched windows with three lights frame the bell enclosure.

The lower church, built at the same time as the upper, has maintained its original structure of four naves

Below left: the apse
Below right: the facade of St. Firmanus Major (San Fermo).

and five apses. It was once entirely frescoed but today there are only a few fragments which, even if rather faded, have however, maintained their notable expressivity.

The cloisters, reached either from the outside or from the upper church, house 18 C. and 19 C. frescoes and a few valuable tombstones.

The inside of the upper church has a single aisle and five apses. A "Crucifixion" attributed to either Altichiero or Turone stands out above the main door. On the right wall, after the frescoes which illustrate the "Martyrdom of the Franciscans in India", one arrives at the Nichesola Chapel which has a beautiful lunette by Domenico Brusasorzi and an altarpiece by Sante Creara. Almost immediately after, is a recently restored fragment of a fresco of angels by Stefano da Verona. The marble pulpit, work of Antonio da Mestre (1396) is surrounded by frescoes by Martino. The splendid urn of the jurist, Barnaba Morano, which he himself had built while he was still alive, is kept in the Brenzoni Chapel (1495).

After Torello Saraina's urn, one comes to the altar the same Saraina had "ordered" with its magnificent altarpiece of the "Trinity and Saints" by Francesco Torbido. Under it is a valuable 15 C "Deposition".

Then follows the Baroque-style Della Torre Altar with Bellotti's altarpiece depicting St. Francis.

At the end, on the right of the cross is the Alighieri Chapel (1541) followed by the Chapel of the Dying with a "Crucifixion" by Brusasorzi. The presbitery, with a 16 C choir, accommodates the Slaves' Altar with the relics of Sts. Firmanus and Rusticus, while the choir has fragments of frescoes including a delicate Madonna of the Sienese school.

On the left wall, St. Anthony's chapel shows an important altarpiece by Liberale (15 C.) and on the arm of the cross vault one can admire frescoes of the Giotto school. A large room on the side accommodates della Torre's prestigious mausoleum - a Renaissance masterpiece by Paduan, Andrea Riccio.

The 17 C. altar erected by the Carpenters' Guild highlights an altarpiece by Turchi. Then one arrives at the Blessed Sacrament Chapel which has a masterpiece by Caroto. Finally, above the side entrance, let your eyes rest on the "Crucifixion" of the school of Altichiero before leaving.

Outside once again, continue left along Stradone San Fermo. After admired the 18 C MURARI DELLA CORTE BRA' palace in the side street, Via Flagini, one stays on the main road and passes a number of magnificent homes: the PALMARINI residence at number 12; the 16 C. BEVILACQUA - LAZISE palace at number 14; the DELLA TORRE palace at number 13 and then one sees the Church of ST. PETER INCARNATED on the left.

This church takes its name from the Roman "carnarium" meaning cemetery because it was built on top of one in 955. After the Second World War it was reconstructed,

14 C. "Crucifixion" preserved in the Church of St. Firmanus Major.

Above: the facade of the Scandola home, special for its "puppets".

Below: the Cavalli home decorated with precious frescoes.

being moved back from the road so as to improve road visibility. It is flanked by a 14 C bell-tower and internally, houses a number of masterpieces: a shrine of "the Virgin, Sts. Peter and John with the sculptor" and the "Stigmata of Francis' by Rigino d'Enrico; a 12 C frescoed "Crucifixion" and, in the

apse, a "Madonna and Saints" by Felice Brusasorzi. The area underground houses remains of an earlier, primitive building.

The continuation of this road is called Stradone Maffei and here one passes WORM PALACE (Palazzo dal Verme): a 12 C edifice, rebuilt in the 16 C with a portal worthy of note (work of Domenico da Lugo). It is followed by the RIDOLFI PALACE which is, nowadays, the scientific lycée "A. Messedaglia" and has frescoes By Domenico Brusasorzi in the main hall.

Back in the street of the Church of St. Peter Incarnated, one can walk to the end and in so doing, find oneself in the popular quarter called the Filippini - a zone which is pratically closed in by roads on two sides and the Adige river. This quarter grew as a result of a buoyant economy and historically, its activities depended exclusively on the river; hence it remained extraneous from Roman urban planning.

After passing the CAVALLI HOME on the left, with its facade depicting allegorical and mythological scenes (by Nicolò Giolfino), one penetrates the area, walking through alleys full of ancient homes and arrives at an ex-slaughterhouse (now a craft center) and the churches, Saint Firmanus Minor and the Philippines (1777) and at the end the CUSTOMS HOUSE built in the mid-18 C. as a junction for land-river commerce. What was the Customs House for lend trade (1753) is now used by the Superintendency of Art and Historic Places while opposite, on the banks of the Adige is the Customs House for goods travelling by river, built in 1792.

Having passed the former slaughterhouse, one comes out in via Pallone, an important arterial road which is flanked on one side by the wall which marked the

boudary of Visconti's "city", and return to the intersection with Stradone Maffei. Veer left and walk along via Tazzoli; at the end, turn into via leoncino to admire a number of elegant palaces: the 15 C MALFER HOME with rooms decorated by Farinati, the AMISTA' home built on Ronzani's design; the SEREGO home designed by Luigi Trezza and opposite, at number 16, the Renaissance-style ALBERTINI Palace. It is now worth detouring slightly for around the corner in via San Cosimo it is difficult not to notice the 16 C SCANDOLA PALACE, popularly known as "The Puppets" because of the caryatids which adorn it.

Back in via Leoncino note the Gothic-style PEREZ Palace, the DIONISI and ERBISTI PALACES (numbers 8 and 6), works of Cristofoli and the home of the prestigious Agricultural Academy. The latter is decorated impressively internally.

Moving towards the Arena again, one comes across ST. NICHOLAS' CHURCH in the square of the same name (piazza San Nicolò). It is the church of the Theatines. Of its original structure only part of the 12 C crypt remains. The actual edifice (1672-83) was designed by Celio Pellesina who adapted its former primitive orientation. The exterior

Above: the entrance to the Land Custom House.

was embellished by the facade taken from St. Sebastian's (which was destroyed), and it has weighty, Ionic, fluted semi-columns - the work of unknown sculptors. Left incomplete by the Jesuits, the project was brought to conclusion by Barbieri. Internally, the church has one large central aisle. The side chapels are adorned by numerous masterpieces - mainly 17 C and 18 C - by Ludovico Dorigny, Simone Brentana, Giuseppe Lonardi, Alessandro Marchesini, Santo Prunato, Antonio Balestra, Antonio Giarola and Orbetto.
The SANSEBASTIANI PALACE

Below: where ships once berthed in front of the Water Customs House.

stands to the right of the church. It is better known as the Diamond Palace (1582) because of the ashlar work on its facade. It was destroyed during the war but then faithfully reconstructed.

Before entering via Mazzini one passes another church on the right, in via Scala: ST. MARY DELLA SCALA (of the Scaligers). It was built in 1324, renovated a century later and then had to be partially reconstructed after World War II. It is full of treasures such as "Pentecost" and the "Madonna of Mercy" by Nicolò Giolfino; "Madonna of Grace" by Turone; the "Crucifixion" by Giovanni Badile

Facing: the beginning of via Mazzini.

Below: the Church of St. Mary of the Scaligers houses precious frescoes.

painted in the lunette of Filippo Guantieri's arch (1430); an "Assumption" by Felice Brusasorzi; "Our lady and the Seven Foundation Members of the Order of the Servants of Mary" by Pietro Rotari. However, probably the most valuable works are the "Stories of St. Jerome" (1443-44) by Giovanni Badile - an exceptional example of the international Gothic Style.

Via Mazzini is a street lined with prestigious shops which tempt the local and tourist alike. Gian Galeazzo Visconti had it constructed to link the Market Square with the Brà, but it was rebuilt in the 19 C. On the corner house at the beginning of the street one can see 17 C. frescoes of the "Annunciation" and "Resurrection" and facing is a column which is dominated by a Gothic shrine sculpted on all four sides, depicting a Madonna with Saints. Number 19 also has 17 C. frescoes on its wall. Then stroll on past the shop-windows.

To finish-off the walk it would be a salutary experience to deviate off via Mazzini and into a lane called "Scudo di Francia" to stop at number 3, the BOTTEGA DEL VINO. After a break, veer back into via Mazzini, turn right and within two minutes one is once more at the beginning of via Cappello with the majestic piazza delle Erbe on the left.

The "Bottega del vino" (literally, wine shop) is a characteristic place of long-standing renown praised, even, by the German, Hans Barth in his celebrated "Spiritual Guide to Italian Pubs". The visitor walks in and is immediately struck by the furniture which is a pleasant mix of Italian and Bavarian styles. The wines served are the best but the beer is also excellent - and the visit is complete with the consumption of snacks and rustic dishes.

What fascinates the new-comer, though, is the vivacious atmosphere which pervades the rooms, always buzzing with a continuous coming and going of groups of young (and not so young) Veronese and foreigners who frequently enjoy late night sittings, chatting and tasting the best of Verona's wines: undoubtedly savouring an evening out of the ordinary.

FIUME ADIGE

Ponte Pietra

Ponte Garibaldi

Riva Battello

P.za Duomo

V. Cappelletta

V. Duomo

Via Garibaldi

V. Ponte Pietro

V. Pigna

V. Forti

V. D. Bassi

V. Rosa

C.so S. Anastasia

V. Sottoriva

V. Trota

P.za Signori

P.za Erbe

P.za Indipendenza

Via Cairoli

Via Nizza

Ponte Nuovo

Via Stella

V. Cappello

Via Amanti

Lungadige Rubele

FIUME ADIGE

Ponte Nuovo

FROM PIAZZA DEI SIGNORI TO THE CATHEDRAL

**Piazza dei Signori (of the Lords)
- Arch of Torture - Old Church of St. Mary and the
Scaliger Tombs - via Sottoriva
- Church of St. Anastasia - Stone Bridge
- Bishop's Palace - Cathedral
- Church of St. John at the Font
- St. Helen's Church - Diocesan Library
- Via Garibaldi**

*This itinerary , although shorter than the preceding ones,
covers one of the most characteristic zones of the centre.
After walking through the Lords' Square and admiring the
Scaliger tombs, one walks down to the river and follows it
round, passing through streets and quarters which were once
strongly dependent on it.
And so, from via Sottoriva, an ancient river port, one passes
the majestic Basilica of St. Anastasia and looks up to St.
Peter's Castle on the hill and across to the pinkish Ponte
della Pietra (literally, stone bridge) which was the Roman
city's link with the Adige Valley. Continuing on, parallel to
the river, one enjoys views down alleyways alternated with
wide open spaces and inevitably arrives at the Cathedral, the
heart of Veronese Catholicism, where a cluster of ancient
churches are "crowned" by the dominating Cathedral.*

Passing through the Costa Arch behind the bussling Market Square (piazza delle Erbe), one arrives at the timidly, half-hidden LORDS' SQUARE which is popularly known as DANTE SQUARE. Not large but of harmonious proportions and artistically rich, it is called the city's drawing-room. Ugo Zannoni's statue of a thoughtful Dante (1865) stands in the middle while the surrounding buildings are almost all palaces which were built during the Scaliger epoch (14 C.) and historically important for the political and judical power they once embodied, for this square was, in reality, the administrative centre of the dominion. The characteristic arches which overhang the lanes help to create harmony and continuity notwithstanding the

The monument to Dante in the centre of the Piazza dei Signori.

variety of architectural styles. The first turning on the right after the Costa Arch, takes one into the Old Market Court and then into Dante Alighieri Street where recent digs have brought to light traces of the Roman decuman gate and axis. The street separates the former Municipal Chambers (palazzo del Comune) from the CAPTAIN'S PALACE, already the Courthouse, erected by Cansignorio della Scala (=Scaliger) above pre-existing houses in 1363. The facade which faces the square has an elegant portal by Sanmicheli. The internal courtyard is decorated by the loggia "Zaccaria Barbaro" (1476) with a three-storey arcade. On the side which leads to Independence Square, one passes the Baroque-style BOMBERS' GATE (1687) designed by Miglioranzi according

to the wish of the Bombers Regiment who had their offices in the nearby Governor's garden. It is adorned with bas-reliefs depicting fighting equipment and military emblems. Maintenance work carried out in the courtyard brought to the surface artefacts from the Medieval period and structures dating back to 1 A.D. The eastern side of the square is delimited by the ARCH OF TORTURE, so-called because in the 16 C instruments of torture then currently in use were hung up there. The arch connected the Captain's Palace with the Questura-Police headquarters (or the Governor or Cangrande). This was the home of the Scaligers and later that of the city's mayor. Built between the end of the 12 C and the beginning of the 13 C., it has, however, undergone extensive restoration over the centuries and more recently in 1929-30. The mansion hosted among others, the exiled Dante and Giotto.

The courtyard has a two-storey loggia and a 14 C. well curb which was taken from the Paletta palace. Just as elegant is the LOGGIA OF THE COUNCILLORS (1476-93) which takes up the north-east side of the square. It was built to accommodate the City Council and it is one of the finest examples of Veronese Renaissance architecture. What makes the structure appear light and delicate is the colour of marble used and the slender columns and capitals. The upper storey is supported by eight large Roman arches placed on a marble baluster and scanned by pilasters which frame four windows with two lights surmounted by a semi-circular tympanum decorated with griffons and mermaids which hold up the city's coat-of-arms. Statues of illustrious Veronese (Catullus, Pliny, Emilio Macro, Vitruvius and Cornelius Nepote) complete the structure and together with the various coloured marble highlight, even further, the linear aspect of the edifice. The architect is unknown. For many years it was

The City Council Loggia is in typical Renaissance architecture. Adjoining it is the old Police Headquarters in the Piazza dei Signori.

A foreshortening of the Piazza dei Signori showing the statue of Girolamo Fracastoro.

wrongly thought to be Frà Giocondo. We know, though, that the statues were the work of the stone-cutters, Alberto and Antonio da Milano; the windows with two lights by Domenico da Lugo and Matteo Panteo; the upper pilasters by Modesto, and the frame was most probably the work of Domenico da Lugo and Mazola. The paintings conserved in the hall are worth seeing, too. Another arch, adorned with the statue of Girolamo Fracastoro (work of Danese Cattaneo, 1559) connects

Among all the strange or wonderful customs and events which this square has witnessed over the centuries, there are two curiosities which render this place even more characteristic: the lion's mouth which stands neglected in a corner of the PALAZZO DEL COMUNE (Municipal Chambers) and the sphere which Girolamo Fracastoro is holding in his hand.
The lion's mouth is one of many which the Venetian Empire (known as the Serenissima) had placed in the city in various locations to take in the secret denunciations of illegal acts against the Republic. It was an opening carved into a stone fixed in a wall where the informer could insert accusatory messages. Obviously these denunciations were read cautiously because they often presented a useful opportunity for the delivery of infamy gratis. What is clear, however, is that this method worked, but the executor made sure he chose the right moment to carry out his duty. He generally moved at night when there were shadows to help him. Legendary, instead, is the belief (and still today the Veronese turn their eyes to Heaven and tend to move to the opposite side) that Girolamo Fracastoro, whose statue dominates the arch between Piazza dei Signori and via Fogge, will drop the sphere onto the head of the first just man who passes under the arch. To date this common credence has never materialised: it would be easy to comment...
Finally, the café, "Dante" deserves a brief mention. It is probably the most prestigious café in Verona and all the city's most talented citizens have, at one time or other, used it as a salon. Despite many ups and downs over the years it is still in business.

the loggia to the CASA DELLA PIETA' (Charity house), while the square is closed at the back by the Domus Mercatorum (Merchants' house) which was rebuilt during the Serenissima (Venetian Dominance) in 1659 and given the name, the JUDGES' PALACE. The statues of Cardinal Enrico Noris (by Domenico dall'Aglio) and Scippione Maffei (by Giovanni Finali - 1756) are sculpted on the sides of the palace.

The ARCH OF TORTURE at the back of the square takes one to the Scaliger cemetery (better known as the ARCHE SCALIGERE) and the adjoining old CHURCH OF ST. MARY. The Arche is one of the city's most important artistic-historical monuments (in front of the Prefecture). Its date of origin is uncertain: some think it was built as early as the 7 C. but its documented existence only begins in the 9 C. and we know that in 1185 the Patriarch of Aquileia reconsecrated it in a solemn ceremony. About one hundred years later, the Scaliger rulers began to consider it their place of worship and to transform the church square into their family cemetery. At that time (13 C. - 14 C.) the edifice had already taken on its present Romanesque appearance and the small bell-tower, with its alternating layers of tufa and brick, has remained unaltered. The church has, however, been altered: especially in 1329 when Cangrande I had the arch modified. After the Scaligers no longer ruled the city this arch was demolished and the architecture changed according to Baroque tastes (C. 1630) It was only in 1827 that careful restoration work brought the church back to its original style. Internally, the church has one nave and two aisles and also three apses. There are few important artworks: a few early 13 C frescoes and a piece of black and white mosaic flooring, perhaps

10C. The tombstone on the walls are more interesting: one, sculpted by Gotifredo, documents the reconsecration of the church in 1185. The Scaliger tombs are highly expressive in their Gothic form, especially so are those of Cangrande I, Cansignorio and Mastino II. This cemetery is enclosed in a superb wrought-iron gate of the Middle Ages. The gate has the family crest engraved on it: a ladder (scala). Mastino I was buried in 1277 after having been barbarously knifed, according to legend, by the current site of the Mazzanti well when returning home from an amorous meeting. His body lies in the first sarcophagus on the right near the

An evocative view of the Scaliger tombs (Arche Scaligere) laced with spires which enclose statues and arches.

external left-side wall of the church. Afterwards, a majestic, sculpted tomb received, in 1301, the mortal remains of Alberto I and just three years later, those of his son, Bartolomeo I. Walking on, with the Scaliger tombs on the right, one arrives at the street, via Arche Scaligere. Turn right and after one hundred metres one comes across a stone tablet on a house with a quote from Shakespeare inscribed on it. This old house, with ivy growing everywhere, is presumed to be the Montecchi house, the home of Romeo, Juliet's lover. It is a brick house adorned with a Romanesque portal and

The tomb of Cangrande I della Scala is incorporated into the old St. Mary's Church.

irregularly-spaced merlons on top. Inside, there is a small courtyard in early Middle Ages-style of architecture. At the end of this street one looks across to two squares - INDEPENDENCE AND VIVIANI - and it would be difficult not to notice the large CENTRAL POST OFFICE (1930; work of Ettore Fagiuoli). Instead of stopping here, turn left and follow the road going towards the river, almost to the end. On the right is the old Pescheria: from 1462-68 it was a meat market, then we are not sure; however, in the 19 C its function changed to that of fish market, hence the name. On the left one enters VIA SOTTORIVA - one of the historical arteries of the city. In ancient times the Roman river port was probably here and later, the porticoes were built to aid the intense activity of loading and unloading goods transported along the Adige. Nowadays, this street has many antique shops but this new designation has not discouraged or threatened the survival of one of the most celebrated osterias in Verona: the "Osteria Sottoriva". The street ends at a corner which is dominated by the BASILICA OF ST. ANASTASIA, one of Verona's most important churches. Its rebuilding began in 1290 when the Dominicans built over a pre-existing small church. Despite being dedicated to St. Peter, the Martyr this basilica has continued to be known by the name of its predecessor, St. Anastasia. The brick facade has never been finished, but worth noting is the portal with a window with two lights which has been attributed to Pietro da Perlezza (1462). The lunette houses frescoes painted by the school of Stefano da Zevio. On the left of the facade is the tomb of Guglielmo di Castelbarco which serves as a link between the ex-Dominican monastery and the small St. George's Church which is a contemporary of the Basilica and

There were once many meeting places of a relaxed and casual nature for those who came up the river and berthed at the beach called Sabbionara on the right bank of the Adige in the stretch between Pietra Bridge and New Bridge (ponte Nuovo). The street SOTTORIVA was a unique sight for one side was lined with pubs and inns, interrupted only by the two intersecting side streets which ran down to the river, and the other was lined with stables (under the porticoes) all the way to Gatto Lane, near the Basilica of St. Anastasia. In the middle, out in the open, one saw vehicles for the transport of every kind of thing imaginable: animals, goods or people. Boatmen, dealers and millers formed a heterogenous crowd in perpetual movement for trade.

This collection of humanity which shouted, discussed, bargained and swapped goods also needed somewhere to still the the pangs of hunger and thirst. To meet this demand a large number of hostels opened up along this street and many places became famous for their menu: tongue with pearà (a typical Veronese sauce), or turkey wings and Valpolicella wine, or lasagne mixed with Bardolino wine. Adventurers squeezed into the pub which best satisfied their taste and carried out their business between one course and another.

After the disastrous flooding of the Adige in September, 1882 Sottoriva witnessed a slow, inexorable decline. The street which had once been a colourful confusion of workers and traders was abandoned and warehouses and inns shut down.

Nowadays, unfortunately, few of these traditional eating places exist but one which does - Osteria Sottoriva - still produces traditional dishes at popular prices. The atmosphere of past times returns, however, with the arrival of summer when one can sit outdoors at a rustic table under the porticoes. The local Veronese poet Berto Barbarani, who wrote in dialect, looked for inspiration in the shade of these porticoes and regular customers included the sculptors, Francesco Modena and Egidio Girelli. The painter, Angelo Dall'Oca Bianca was unmistable, too, in his floppy, white hat worn at an angle and moustache like that of a muskateer.

Intellectuals, artists, celebrities and ordinary folk mixed freely, exchanging opinions.

If, however, the past was glorious, the present is certainly not to be scorned. A heterogeneous clientele still squabbles over the tables right from the morning, there to "marry" fresh white or pungent red wines with a salt-and-peppered egg or a pre-lunch snack. Foreigners did not take long to find this inviting spot and they stop to mix casually with the locals, at times for lengthy periods.

Between one glass and another they exchange a few words, enough to establish a rapport which serves to keep them there even longer, thereby giving the host an incessant stream of glasses to fill and ashtrays to empty. To testify to the "bounty" of the wine, this pub has even had the honour of appearing (with photo and commentary) in the well-known American magazine "Esquire".

A foreshortening of the porticoes in via Sottoriva.

houses valuable frescoes such as Altichiero's "Crucifixion" and a lively "Allegory" by Falconetto. The elegant bell-tower was constructed in the 14 C. The Basilica has a nave and two aisles, separated by twelve marble columns and five apses in the typical Italian Gothic style. The ceiling has finely decorated bohemian vaults. At the base of the first columns on the left and right as one enters the basilica, are two holy water fonts. The caryatids which hold them up are popularly known as dwarfs. The older one (1495) is that on the left and was the work of the stonecarver Gabriele Caliari, father of the famous painter, Paolo (better known as Paolo Veronese). The one on the right, called Pasquino because it was placed in the basilica on Easter (Pasqua) Sunday, 1591 was the work of Paolo Orefice. Moving along the right wall, after the fifth altar is a chapel with a wooden 15 C. Crucifix, of intense expressivity.

A fine view of the exterior of the Basilica of St. Anastasia which stands out from the surrounding buildings for the warmth of colour of the brick.

The wooden sculpture "Ecce Homo" in a niche on the right is worth noting. On the left wall notice the Pietà group and a Gothic tomb. At the seventh altar called the Centrego, there is a precious altarpiece by Girolamo dai Libri, depicting the "Madonna on the Throne between Sts. Augustine and Thomas". In the fully frescoed Cavalli Chapel one can admire Liberale's altarpiece with miniatures; Altichiero's "Virgin on the Throne" on the right and the fresco depicting Federico Cavalli's grave painted by Stefano da Zevio. Then follows the famous Pellegrini Chapel on whose external arch Pisanello's fresco of St. George and the Princess once stood. It was later moved and is nowadays found in the sacristy. Other precious works include the terracotta figures attributed to Michele da Firenze; Avanzo's fresco showing "Pellegrini's sarcophagus" and "De Bibra's Monument". The right wall

The facade of the Basilica of St. Anastasia.

of the presbytery is highlighted by the large fresco of the "Last Judgment" by Turone and opposite, Giambono's "Annunciation".

Nani di Bartolo (1429) was the artist behind "Cortesia Serego's Mausoleum". Before coming to the Giusti Chapel, one passes the Salerni Chapel - a small jewel which was built around the turn of the 15 C and attributed to Altichiero and Stefano da Zevio. The precious choir which was finely carved in walnut by Master Lorenzo da Santa Cecilia highlights the walls of the Giusti Chapel. The two windows of 1460 are the oldest windows in Verona.

And, of course, look at Pisanello's masterpiece which has already been mentioned. Along the left aisle the altar of the Chapel of the Holy Rosary has a precious "Virgin and Child" by Lorenzo Veneziano and in the lunette, a work by Orbetto. The organ, built in 1625, has at times been badly tampered with. It immortalises figures of pontiffs and Dominican saints. A small Renaissance masterpiece is the altar of the Holy Spirit, the work of Pietro da Portezza. Golfino's canvas deserves a mention, too. Behind St. Anastasia's one can cross the square, Brà Molinari (brà from the latin "braida" meaning

The holy water font which rests on the dwarf's (Pasquino's) shoulders in the basilica of St. Anastasia.

Like many other churches, the Basilica of Saint Anastasia also opened up onto the via Postumia. In this area Theodoric, King of the Ostrogoths, had had two small churches built: one called St. Anastasia, the other St. Remigio. It is a curious fact that the present basilica is officially called St. Peter's, after a Veronese martyr who was killed on 29 April, 1252 and elevated to sainthood by Pope Innocent IV on 24 March, 1253. However, the Veronese already used to venerating St. Anastasia continued to call the new building by that time long after the small Theodoric church ceased to exist.

wide space), to stand alongside the long walls of the left bank of the Adige to admire the magnificent view of ST. PETER'S CASTLE (an ex-Austrian barracks) and below it, the ROMAN THEATRE with the CHURCH OF STS. SIRO AND LIBERA slightly above it. On the left the ancient stone bridge resists the coursing of the Adige and the scene is framed by the surrounding hills. Then, proceeding along via Ponte Pietra, one comes to the Giusti palace (on the left) with its friezes dating back to the first half of the 15 C., while number 2, via Santa Felicita was the Nichesola home, Romanesque in origin. Other buildings, full of history and restructured more than once, face onto adjoining alleyways. According to the now dead, but former historian, Gino Beltramini it seems possible that the nucleus of buildings in via Cappelletta could well have been the traditional residence of the Capulets, one of the two families implicated in the tragedy of Romeo and Juliet. At the end of via Ponte Pietra at number 23-25 is a house

The Roman bridge della Pietra (of stone) crosses the Adige in one of the most enchanting points of the city.

with an important 16 C. frieze at the top. Here the various sequences involved in processing pork and milk are described. Almost opposite is the Roman bridge della Pietra (of stone), the city's oldest bridge. The monumental work leads to one of the most enchanting corners of Verona. It was constructed in 89 A.D. during the Roman Republic but its original name is not known. The name by which it is known nowadays was adopted during the Middle Ages. Over the centuries continual restructuring modified its appearance, each intervention reducing its Roman aspect even more until 1945 when the bridge was mined by the retreating German troops. Between 1957-59 it was reconstructed as faithfully as possible to the original, and today it retains its fascination both for the diversity of materials used and its panoramic position. The two arches on the left of the bridge-those on the side of St. Peter's hill - are from the Roman epoch and were fully restored using masses of original stone salvaged from the river. The three adjoining arches built in brick and stone were added on later, substituting the original Roman ones which had been worn down by the raging river. The central bay and that immediately after had been rebuilt in 1520 by the architect, Antonio Scarpagnino, as testified by an epigraph found on the second arch; while the last arch which leans against the right bank and its nearby tower are a reconstruction carried out in 1298 under the guidance of Alberto I della Scala. Roman construction was innovative and ingenious and dispensed with the architrave so widely used by the Greeks, favouring instead, the round, elongated arch supported by two lateral pilasters which became transformed into the stylistic feature of an arcade. As a memorial of the restoration work carried out

during the years when Verona was a Roman municipality, there is a representation of a fluvial divinity on the second arch on the left. It was placed there to protect the bridge from any impetuous change of course. Back on the right bank, from via Ponte Pietra one continues on to Broilo Square, a romantic oasis in a city which has become "deformed" by the motor-car. The square is dominated by a large 15 C building (extensively restructured in the 19 C.) which houses the APORTIAN KINDERGARTEN AND PRIMARY SCHOOL. Beyond this, a broadening out of spaces which form courtyards and streets leads one to the BISHOP'S PALACE, dated 15 C. but, in fact, of earlier origins. The edifice is enclosed by a battlemented wall. It has a black and white marble portal and a lunette depicting the "Madonna on the Throne with Sts. Peter, Paul and Michael". The

Notwithstanding uncertain dates and few ruins to go by, it is known that there was a second Roman Bridge still open in the late Middle Ages. Construction of an embankment for protection came after the floods of 1882 and it was then that traces of a Roman bridge came to light: a bridge which Biadego had called Postumio after the ancient Roman road. The discovery was interpreted as confirmation of a link with the decuman gate (the east-west axis taken as a line of orientation). The bridge would have been not only bigger than the Pietra (still in existence) but boasted a richer and more elaborate form of architecture. Some researches maintain that it rose at the high ground of Isolo Square. The discovery of ruins is recorded on a stone tablet set into the embankment near the monument to Paolo Veronese.

palace boasts Bishop Ognibene's keep of 1172 and the meeting room is lined with portraits of Veronese bishops by Domenico Brusasorzi. In the Bishop's quarters there is a "Resurrection of Lazarus" (1531) by Francesco Caroto; a "Nativity of Mary", an "Adoration of the Magi" and a "Death of Mary" by Liberale da Verona. This ancient quarter has

Above: the small loggia of the Aportiani Kindergarten.

To the left: the Bishop's Palace whose origins are pre-15 C.

been the home of the Church right from the early Middle Ages. It unites, in a series of monuments, an artistic-cultural tradition which is truly unique. The CHURCH OF ST. JOHN AT THE FONT adjoins the Bishop's Palace. Following on one sees the majestic apse of the Cathedral and opposite, surrounded by a large garden, the AVANZI HOUSES - built in the 14 C on a structural design of the preceding century. Continuing along the right side of the Cathedral one passes the small Roman-Gothic Church of St. Peter in Archivolt which is nowadays used as a parish meeting room. Cathedral Square is where all the alleys, lanes, roads and wide spaces meet and in so doing, focus one's attention on the beautiful but intricate facade of the edifice. The Cathedral, dedicated to St. Mary Matrix, was probably built on a pre-existent Roman temple which was then followed by a big early-Christian basilica in the 5 C. The oldest architectural forms date back to the early 9 C and it seems

A striking view of the Cathedral and the bell-tower which flanks it.

that the construction was promoted by Archdeacon Pacifico. Subsequent Romanesque additions in the 12 C were probably the work of Giolfino. The facade reveals a change of styles: without doubt, the lower part is more remarkable. Giolfino's two-tiered, marble gabled arch is supported by columns leaning on winged griffons. The guardians of the temple, the champions Orlando and Oliviero stand on the sides of the portal. The gabled arch is adorned with the sculptures of many evangelical subjects, most of them by Nicolò. A small, 12 C. gabled arch protects the side entrance on the south side of the building. The bell-tower has never been completed at the top, but its foundation at least, is said to be the work of sanmicheli. The main apse is worth noting for its entire tufa construction and floral-motif strip decoration at the top. Internally, the Italian-Gothic style prevails: one central nave with two side aisles and five bays divided by eight red marble columns. There are

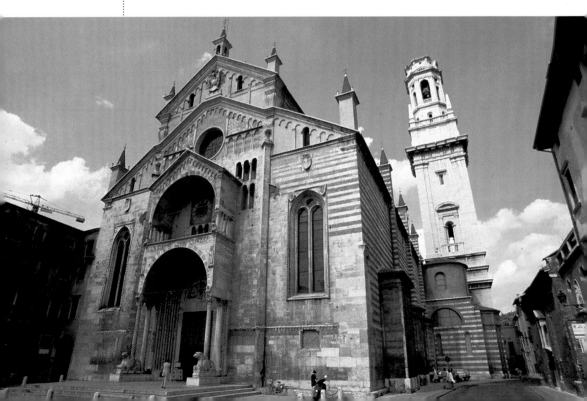

four side chapels along each side: the two major ones give the church the form of a cross. The first chapel on the right reveals frescoes by Falconetto on the outside and late 14 C statues of "Jesus risen from the dead" and Sts. Peter and Paul - of unknown authorship. The second has an altarpiece of the "Holy Family with the Magi", attributed to Liberale da Verona, and beside this, various saints depicted by Giolfino. Also by Giolfino, "Jesus is taken down from the Cross" in the lunette. The holy water font which is near the south door dates back to the 12 C. The third chapel, also decorated on the outside by Falconetto, houses Cignaroli's "Transfiguration (1741). After the Baroque fourth altar, look at the choir on the right with the "Assumption" by Biagio Falceri painted on the doors. Pope Lucio III's sepulchral seal can be seen on the left of the organ. One has now arrived at the south apse where the relics of St. Agatha are kept in a marble urn (1353), work of an unknown craftsman. Under the altar table is the urn of St. Mary, the Consoler. The architecture on the exterior is said to be that of

Domenico da Lugo, 15 C. The presbytery is demarcated by Sanmicheli's grand semi-circular construction of marble arches which rest on a balustrade (16 C.) and on the door Giobatta da Verona engraved a Christ in bronze. The

Above: a detail of the portal of the Cathedral.

Below: a detail of the gabled arch.

two sides apses are also by the same artist while the vault, basin and triumphal arch have been attributed to Francesco Torbido using a design of Giulio Romano (Raphael's favourite protégé). There is a valuable "Annunciation with the prophets, Isaiah and Ezechiel" painted on the triumphal arch. Gilberti donated the six superb bronze candelabra which can be seen on the high altar and there are also two valuable lecterns in carved wood. The chapel on the left is dedicated to three former bishops of Verona: Annone, Valente and Verecondo and has a beautiful "Jesus is taken down from the Cross" by Morone, while above, the doors of the other big organ were painted by Brusasorzi. Immediately after this, is one of the few works by Giovanni Caroto "Madonna between Sts. Martin and Stephen".

The Canonicate Palace is the home of the Cathedral Library.

The Cartolari Chapel, dedicated to St. Michael, the Archangel has Francesco Morone's "Birth of John the Baptist" while the Chapel of St. Lawrence and the Assumption boasts a beautiful column-altar (masterpiece of Sansovino) and a famous "Assumption" by Tiziano Vecellio which is considered one of Verona's finest paintings.

At the back along the left wall a door leads one out of the Cathedral and into an area which is extraordinarily rich in archaeological finds. As well as a small nave which is still intact and links the Cathedral to ST. HELEN'S CHURCH, there is a lot of evidence of the pre-existent early-Christian basilica and from here one can also have access to "ST. JOHN AT THE FONT", a Romanesque Baptistry built at about the same time as the Cathedral (8 C. or 9 C.) but reconstructed in 1125 after the devastating earthquake of 1117. The facade is in tufa and the apses have 8 C. columns and conserve 14 and 15 C. frescoes. But the real jewel is, undoubtedly, the baptismal font (early 13 C. which has eight scenes from the life of Christ carved on it. The craftsman remains unknown. Leaving the Cathedral, one follows the left wall and arrives at ST. HELEN'S COURT with the church of the same name. Outside the church is a small 14 C. portico. Archeological digs have demonstrated that the church built in 813 on the orders of Archdeacon Pacifico and reconstructed three hundred years later was, in fact, built on top of an early-Christian basilica which had, in turn, been constructed above an even older one dating back to the reign of Constantine, 306-337. Internally, to be noted are: a polychromatic triptych depicting a "Madonna with Sts. John, the Baptist and John, the Evangelist with a holy man"; a 15 C. wooden choir and a canvas of the "Madonna and Child with Sts. Helen

and George" by Felice Brusasorzi. It is said that it was in this church in 1320 that Dante discussed the Quaestio (Question) of water and earth. The Cathedral's Romanesque cloister (1140) is opposite St. Helen's. A two-tiered construction in Verona Red marble, it was built on top of a Paleo-Christian basilica and much

Above: the two tiers of twin-columned arches which line one side of the Cathedral Cloister.

Below: a detail of the baptismal font which is housed in the Cathedral.

In the 1924 the palaeographer, Luigi Schiaparelli, recovered the oldest written document in vulgar Italian in existence, in the Cathedral Library of Verona. This writing consisted of two lines of verse composed between the end of the 8 C. and the beginning of the 9 C., and was found at the top of a page of a Mozarabic prayerbook.

The lines read:

Se pareba boves alba pratalia araba
e albo versorio teneba e negro semen seminaba...

and traslated as follows:

"The oxen where pushed on to plough the virgin field
Bearing a white tray and sowing black seeds".

The first interpretation was philological: Tarmassia read nothing more than the opening of a peasant song in these marginal notes. Or perhaps they were the first couplet of a very old, popular Georgic song. Linguistically-speaking he thought he recognized one of the first attempts of rhythmic poetry which distantly heralded the dawn of the new vernacular.

Vincenzo De Bartholomaeis was of another opinion: he belived that this was not in rough Latin but rather semi-vernacular. Roberto Viscardi also merits a mention for having seriously considered the question apart from philological dissertation.

What is more important - and interesting - is the content of the verse. It is not, in fact, a sing-song but rather a riddle in which the act of writing is described: comparing the action of ploughing to that of write. The *boves* are the fingers which guide the pen; the *alba pratalia* is the white parchment; the *albo versorio* the feather-pen and the *negro semen* the black ink.

Interesting, too, are the various opinions about the nature and origin of the text. It has been found that this Veronese riddle is known in other parts of Italy, albeit with a number of variations which do not, however, modify the substance to any extent. As for the author, it is thought to have been a cleric of the great Veronese Cathedral chapter. Confirmation of the cultural extraction of the author is the fact that it is the same hand which afterwards added a prayer in correct Latin: *Gratias tibi agimus omnipotens sempiterne deus*, turning the words into verse according to the rules of the distinguished Medieval-Latin clerical traditions.

The Montolti Rotari Palace is one of the most beautiful buildings found in the narrow streets around the Cathedral complex.

evidence still remains. The CANONICATE PALACE is in the Cathedral Square. Rebuilt after the bombings of World War II, it is the home of the CATHEDRAL LIBRARY and almost 1500 years old. The library's oldest manuscript bears the date 517, the height of the period of Ostrogoth domination. Possibly the most important library of its kind in Europe, it has always been considered an international font of knowledge. To ascertain the exact number of precious miniatures and ancient manuscripts in this enormous collection is difficult. However, some of them have been fundamental in interpreting the birth of the Italian language and therefore, a visit here is a must for researchers and the curious. The same building hosts the CANONICAL ART MUSEUM which has masterpieces of great value. Before leaving this zone completely, it is worth roaming around the alleyways and narrow side streets to look at some of the old mansions decorated with friezes and other masterpieces. In via Duomo take a look at the MANUELI PALACE at number 15, the MONTOLTI ROTARI PALACE at number 10, the GUARIENTI PALACE opposite the FORTI PALACE and the RAVIGNANI PALACE. Probably of Roman origin is a sculpture of a pine-cone (pigna) and so it is not surprising that the street was named after the sculpture placed at the corner. At the intersection of via Verità and via Forti one sees, on the left, the EMILEI-FORTI PALACE built during the 18 C. by Ignazio Pellegrini. It was here that Napoleon Bonaparte stayed during his Italy Campaign, 1796-97. Nowadays, it houses the Museum of the Italian Risorgimento and the important GALLERY OF MODERN AND CONTEMPORARY ART. In the last decade this gallery has hosted international exhibitions of high quality. If one walks away from the Cathedral, however, and follows Stradone (literally, big road) Archdeacon Pacifico, one can still see a fresco depicting St. John, the Baptist on the first house on the left. Then follows the Paletta Palace with its magnificent 16 C. portal (work of Domenico da Lugo), while on the right stands the 15 C Ferrari (ex-Murari) Palace. At the end of the road one arrives at via Garibaldi which is full of big palaces, the most imposing being the grand MINISCALCHI PALACE built in the 19 C. Follow this road to the end and arrive back at the Market Square again.

Left: the Roman sculpture of a pine-cone which gave its name to the street.

Below: the Manueli Palace is one of the oldest and most valuable homes in via Duomo.

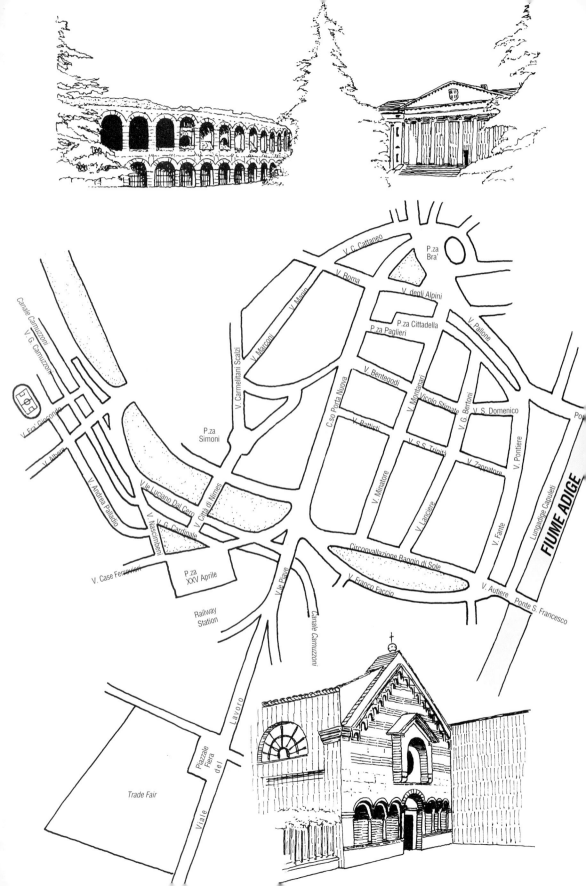

Canale Camuzzoni
V. G. Camuzzoni
Canale Camuzzoni

V. Fra' Giocondo

V. Albaro

V. Andrea Palladio

V.le Luciano Dal Cero

V. G. Cardinale

V. Mascimbeni

V. Case Ferrovieri

V. Carmelitani Scalzi

V. Marconi

V. Mario

V. C. Cattaneo

V. Roma

P.za Bra'

V. degli Alpini

P.za Cittadella

P.za Paglieri

V. Pallone

V. Bentegodi

V. Montanari

Vicolo Stimate

V. G. Bertoni

V. S. Domenico

C.so Porta Nuova

V. Battisti

V. S.S. Trinità

V. Zappatore

V. Pontiere

Po

P.za Simoni

V. Città di Nîmes

P.za XXV Aprile

V.le Piave

V. Minatore

V. Lanciere

V. Fante

Lungadige Capuleti

FIUME ADIGE

Circonvallazione Baggio di Sole

V. Franco Faccio

V. Autiere

Ponte S. Francesco

Railway Station

Canale Camuzzoni

Viale   Lavoro

Piazzale Fiera del

Trade Fair

From New Gate (Porta Nuova) to the Arena

Trade Fair - Railway station
- Corso (Avenue) Porta Nuova - St. Luke's Church
- Cittadella - Holy Trinity Church
- Church of St. Francis on the Avenue (al Corso)
- Juliet's Tomb - via Pallone
- Monumental Cemetery - Brà Square
- Maffei Epigraphic Museum
- Philharmonic Theatre - Arena - Town Hall
- Palace of the Great Guard (Gran Guardia)

This is the route for all those who leave the motorway at the Verona South exit to arrive in the city. A number of small streets lead one directly into the Scaliger centre within a short space of time. Convenient, too, are the carparks which are positioned just beyond the city walls and also the central carpark at Cittadella Square. This tourist itinerary begins at Porta Nuova (New Gate) and winds along and around the avenue of the same name finishing at Brà Square with a look at the Arena. Topographically speaking, it is a linear route but it also includes detours to take in various monuments which mark important historical and artistic moments in the history of the city.

*The facade of Porta
Nuova facing
inwards towards
the city centre. Its
original design by
Sanmicheli was
extensively altered
by the Austrians.*

On leaving the motorway at the Verona South exit, one passes through the outer suburb which hosts the Trade Fair and after going over the flyover, one sees the Scaliger city in all its splendour opening up before one's eyes. Beforehand, however, one circumnavigates the intersection at NEW GATE (Porta Nuova), the work of Sanmicheli. Built between 1533-46 the construction was altered in 1854 during the Austrian occupation. Of the original plan only the central arch enclosed in Doric columns still remains. The Austrian addition changed the internal facade which is in tufa; the new part has the same width as the old but two windows instead of side doors. The Venetian winged lion was sculpted by the Jacobins who, however, removed the Venetian coat-of-arms and substituted it with that of the royal family. The avenue which extends from here to the Brà is the largest road in the old city enclosure. It was projected by Sanmicheli who followed the line of the boundary wall. Nowadays its function is to connect the historic centre with the railway station as quickly and directly as possible. The railway station extends just beyond New Gate and also has the same name: Stazione Porta Nuova. After passing a small park (Valverde) on the left - recently put in order after the bombs buried in it (a legacy of World War II) had been defused - one comes to ST. LUKE'S CHURCH, not far from the entrance to the Brà Square. Rebuilt in 1753, this church houses Claudio Ridolfi's "Guardian Angel" and an "Assumption" by Orbetto. A 14 C. Crucifix hangs on the interior of the outer wall. On the opposite side of the road, there is a small lane, Vicolo Ghiaia which is graced by the small Romanesque church ST. MARY OF THE GRAVEL - a recent object of restoration. Following this lane to the end one arrives in CITTADELLA SQUARE, nowadays only a part of what was once a much more extensive fortification built by Gian Galeazzo Visconti at the end of the 15 C. and

The small church of ST. MARY OF THE GRAVEL can boast an interesting past.

According to tradition Federico Barbarossa, after conquering Milan, imprisoned many noblemen and sent them as hostages to Germany. After years of sufferance they were freed on payment of a ransom: members of the family of the hostages presented themselves before the Emperor dressed simply in white gowns.

After having achieved their objective, neither the ex-prisoners nor their relatives stopped wearing the white habit and in time they founded a religious order called "the Humiliated", whose rule was based on obedience and humility. In Verona, this order established itself near a little chapel dedicated to the Madonna which was situated just outside the big gates of the Brà, a spot where all the sand and gravel which the Adigetto had deposited over the years banked up. The order, which originally imposed a life of poverty, admitted friars, monks and, initially, married people to its community. Contrary to its said intentions, however, it later became one of the richest congregations in Verona. They reached such a position of power that in 1568, they tried to plot against Charles Borromeo, guilty for having attempted to reform the order. Three members of the order were arrested (one of them, from the convent in Verona, succeeded in escaping) and condemned to death. Two years later, in 1570, Pope Pius V suppressed the order!

Below: the facade of the Church of St. Mary of the Gravel.

At the bottom: a colourful panorama of Corso Porta Nuova.

A spectacular view of St. Peter's Castle with the Roman Theatre on the left below.

mantained, afterwards, by the Venetians. Among its uses it offered refuge to the Milanese militia during the insurrection of 1390. This defence complex occupied the territory between Pallone Street and the river: the walls extended from the Adige to New Gate (Porta Nuova), even though there was the road which connected the Brà to New Gate. The majestic MONTANARI PALACE dominates the street of the same name. Giacomo Verità had it built in 1583 but it was raised in 1762. These days it is the home of the Art Academy Cignaroli.

What remains of the Visconti wall in Cittadella Square.

There are few cities like Verona which can boast so many walls and fortifications from various epochs, spanning almost 2,000 years of history. The Borsari and Leoni gates are attractive for being Roman. However, certainly more impressive are the weighty rows of ramparts, rounds and bunkers built by the Venetians and duly reinforced by the Austrians when the city became the main vertex of the Quadruple Alliance (system of defence). Verona was a fortress city then, and for further confirmation one needs only visit the forts and towers which dominate the surrounding hills.

But if the Venetian and Austrian walls are still largely visible and history, therefore, easily able to be read, it is certainly more difficult to interpret the defence system prior to this. Here follows a brief summary of the principal interventions to which the city was subjected from the time of Roman rule to that of the Viscontis (from Milan).

The first fortified wall was not so long and dates back to Roman times. It was probably constructed in the first half of 1 B.C. and its measurements can be deduced from fragments found. The wall began on the left bank of the Adige near the rock, the Roman transformation of the ancient castle buildings on St. Peter's hill. Two great walls extended down from the summit of the high ground: one west of the old stone bridge (the Pietra), the other east of the Postumia bridge. Evidence of this wall exists on the right bank of the river, at the Leoni and Borsari gates and a section of a thick wall found in the streets, Diaz and Leoncino. Also to be remembered is the fact that both these gates were embellished with decorations realised in the first century A.D.

Still during the Roman epoch, in 265, Gallieno reinforced and enlarged the city's defences. In fact, "his" wall is still visible today: in via Leoncino, in the small square behind the Arena, in via Diaz and via Cantone, in the small San Matteo lane and at other points. The walls of the Arena itself, were included in this project of reinforcement.

Theodoric was responsable for the third remake of this Roman wall but, unfortunately, no concrete evidence of this intervention remains except for documentation from chronicles and the celebrated Raterian Iconography, a picture which shows the city as it was in the late Middle Ages. Perhaps the work of King Arduino, the old wall of the area known as Campo Marzio was constructed in 11 C. It was an advanced system of defence, designed with the aim of obstructing Enrico II's imperial troops. More important, instead, was the first and new city boundary wall built on the right bank of the river between 1194 and 1224, much bigger than the Roman-Theodoric one. This wall began near the area of the Scaliger Bridge (at Castelvecchio), followed the Adigetto - a diversion of the Adige, used as a ditch for defence purposes - and then joined the Adige near the Aleardi Bridge. Later Ezzelino reinforced the wall with towers, the most majestic example being the Pentagona by the entrance to Brà Square.

In the 14 C. Alberto and Cangrande della Scala further strengthened the city's defence structures, though still maintaining the old walls. A great Scaliger innovation was the construction of Castelvecchio to satisfy the wishes of Cangrande II (and amply describd in Itinerary I).

Gian Galeazzo Visconti was also responsible for innovation. Suspicious of Veronese loyalty, he had two ingenious structures realized. The first was to construct Cittadella (literally, a small city): an almost-square plan locked in at the west side with another wall and thereby obtaining in this double city boundary, a patrolled walkway which would guarantee his troops a secure passage between Cittadella and Castelvecchio. The second innovation was on the left bank of the Adige where he renovated the so-called Castle of King Theodoric (or St. Peter's) reinforcing it with ten towers and a fort and connecting it with the outermost wall built by his predecessor, Cangrande.

The facade is Sanmichelian in style with windows and arches and a loggia supported by rusticated arches. The courtyard is enclosed by a battlemented wall. By crossing over a small side street one arrives at HOLY TRINITY CHURCH. A Romanesque edifice built by the monks of Vallombrosa around the 11C., it rises up on a piece of high ground which was called, at the time, the Mount of Olives. Notwithstanding the surrounding city traffic, the position of this place of worship is suggestive. The Romanesque covered -in cloister which precedes the church is supported by fine columns of red marble; on the walls there are a number of funereal inscriptions and, on the left, the marble sarcophagus of Antonia, Fregnano da Sesso's daughter. The facade is made up of strata of tufa and brick, highlighted by an elegant gabled arch which encloses a rose window. The monastery door is surmounted by a niche which houses a 14 C. sculpture of the Trinity.

The facade of Holy Trynity Church, striking for its cloister entrance and gabled arch.

The bell-tower, built at the same time as the church, is in the shape of a cone with pinnacles at the corners; the bell enclosure is decorated with windows with three lights articulated by fine twin-columns. Internally, the church has a single nave and three apses. The lunette above the main entrance shows a fresco of God the Father while, on the right, is a (delapidated) "Conversion of St. Paul" by Felice Brusasorzi. Following on there are two canvases: one by Ligozzi (on the right) and one by Domenico Brusasorzi (on the left). The latter is also the author of the two frescoes above the nearby altars: "St. Ursula" (right) and "Marriage of St. Catherine to Jesus and St. Onofrio" (left). The triumphal arch of the presbytery reveals a 14 C. "Annunciation" while, under the arch, one can admire eight saints by Martino da Verona (or Stefano da Zevio). Leave the church and go down via dello Zappatore (of the Hoer). At the intersection of via del Pontiere, turn

left and then turn right into via Franceschine. Here, the STATE ARCHIVES are located: 70,000 volumes and 82,000 parchment papers and documents.

At this point one is near JULIET'S TOMB - site of the final, extreme act of love between the two young lovers. The small chapel opens out into cloisters of the ex-Capuchin Monastery and former CHURCH OF ST. FRANCIS ON THE AVENUE (al Corso). A richly evocative place, it is reached through a short peristyle and then a colonnade which brings one out into the Neo-Classical cloister. Then one goes down a short flight of steps to a basement area where a 14 C. sarcophagus in Verona-red marble lies. Legend has it that this sarcophagus hosts the remains of the young heroine. Thanks to restoration, this site has acquired dignity. However, it seems that for centuries this legendary episode was ignored and neglected. Charles Dickens, the great English novelist, for example, described his experience in Verona in the nineteenth century saying, that after visiting and appreciating the monuments of the Scaliger city, he felt quite disappointed with his visit to the tomb. "I entered via a ramshackle gate which was opened for me by a woman with bright eyes, who was doing her handwashing. She led me along various paths bordered with plants and flowers which produced a beautiful effect. At a certain point she pointed out a kind of drinking trough which the woman with bright eyes, drying her arms with a handkerchief, called the tomb of Juliet, the unlucky one".

"A drinking trough then, an abandoned ruin among the nettle, suitable perhaps for handwashing! Such indifference!" In effect, many years passed before the tomb could have a dignified resting place. The whole site fell into a state of abandonment when the Franciscan nuns left both the church and the convent in 1842, and it was not until the Congregation of Charity arrived,

Frescoes in the dome of the apse in Holy Trinity Church.

The legend of Romeo and Juliet has changed this century and become extremely romantic. The turning point came in 1937 when a letter addressed to Juliet, written by a young person pouring out her heart, arrived from abroad. The custodian of Juliet's house, touched by this gesture of candour, felt he could not deny the writer a reply for she was obviously desperate for advice or perhaps sincerely hoping to get in touch with the Veronese heroine. This was the spark and within just a few decades the volume of correspondence has increased to dizzy proportions: each missive disparate in content but always dealing with that noblest of human sentiments, love.

So, in order to satisfy the needs of lovers all over the world a well-known personage in Verona, the unforgettable Gino Beltramini, took on the task of writing a reply or some advice to all those who sought help from Juliet, thereby consolidating a system of tacit deception (gliding over the fact of her tragic end) which has, therein, elevated her to the position of a new goddess of hard-won love. After the death of Beltramini others took over this job which was becoming more onerous annually owing to the continual increase in the volume of missives: from some in anguish, others wishing to communicate happy resolutions. At the end it was decided to institute a prize: an annual award for the letter which expressed the most sorrowful sentiments. The competition called "Dear Juliet" has recently been won by a 21-year-old French girl for her extremely romantic words. The prize, instituted by Juliet's Club, consists of a gold sculpture (realised by the goldsmith Alberto Zucchetta, on the design of Milo Manara) which depicts a sensuous Juliet leaning dreamily over the balcony towards love.

Other projects, similar to those of the letter but of a more spontaneous and impromtu nature, have been realised in recent years. These have involved the crypt where Juliet's sarcophagus is preserved and the entrance hall to her house.

Everyday people from all over the world leave notes on her tomb asking for her intercession. Others adopt more public methods, inscribing phrases, their signatures and hearts on the walls of the entrance to the courtyard of her house. Here we see a phantasmagoria of signs and colours and the strangest of messages which are engraved month after month, unfortunately eroding the walls - substituting the limestone with messages of supplication. Hence, the house of the unlucky young girl lives again with voices and promises in a continuous spiritual ferment which definitively proves the victory of love over death.

that the sarcophagus was, at least, moved to a sheltered spot: in a colonnade among the ruins of the heavily damaged cloister. Finally, in 1898 the City Council decreed that the "marble" should be given a more dignified environment , but another ten years passed before any concrete move was made: in 1910, on the occasion of the laying of the herma of Shakespeare, the first step was taken to improve the situation but it was only in 1937 that the interventions arrived at a logical conclusion. The final insult to the memory of Juliet were the bombings during World War II, after which she was given her final resting place.

The FRESCO MUSEUM is situated on the opposite side of the courtyard which custodies the tomb. Instituted in 1973, it was named after the art historian, G.B. Cavalcaselle.

Numerous Veronese paintings which came from civic and, above all, religious buildings are exhibited here. By passing through a corridor, one arrives at the CHURCH OF ST. FRANCIS ON THE AVENUE: a 13 C. structure which was reconstructed in 1625 and has been recently restored. In practice, this temple is a continuation of the museum in that it houses important paintings of the Veronese school from various epochs. Back in via del Pontiere one sees ST. DOMINIC'S CHURCH on the right.

Juliet's tomb is conserved in the Capuchin cloister of the ex Church of St. Francis on the Avenue.

Verona's Fair has centuries-old origins. Originally held in the Brà, it was a big market for livestock, hay, straw and timber and known as the Cattle Forum. After various complex historical events, the Senate of the Veneto consented, on 21 January, 1633, to the Fair of Merchandise in Verona. This was to take place in the Brà and its immediate vicinity twice a year, for fifteen days each period.
The first period would begin on 25 April, the second on 25 October.
The inauguration ceremony of this Trade Fair was held on 25 April, 1633 and descriptions recorded are of interest. "The Fair is arranged in three big streets along which 250 well-organised stalls are uniformly placed on both sides, while other sellers and stalls are out of order, full or overflowing with the richest and most specious stuff of every kind... and the site by the old walls is filled with horses and other animals".
The fair remained in the Brà for 80 years, until it was destroyed by fire on 28 October, 1712. Reinstated ten years later, but this time in Campofiore where it remained until 1749, it continued to expand.
In 1822 it returned to the Brà and the first modern trade fair (as we know it today) was inaugurated on 27 September, 1822.
75 years later it was substituted by the Horse Fair which had, over the years, taken on an increasingly set agricultural identity. This (horse) fair has grown to such dimensions that it is nowadays one of the most important of its kind in Europe.

Built between 1536 and 1543, it has, an 18 C. portal with Orazio Marinali's statue of St. Dominic placed above. The interior is Baroque in style (1687) and decorated with a beautiful ceiling which has an "Our Lady in Glory" by Alessandro Marchesini and helpers, and "Stories of the Life of St. Catherine" by Odoardo Perini - author also of the canvas of the "Miracle of St. Dominic".

At this point, one exits and sees the walls of the Scaliger city: the walls which line via Pallone were reinforced by Gian Galeazzo Visconti (end of the 15 C) to defend the city centre. By walking left, one arrives at Brà Square, but before going there, it might be worth digressing to visit the Monumental Cemetery: reached by turning right, following the city wall to the end and crossing the river at the Aleardi bridge. For sometime now the MONUMENTAL CEMETERY has been of interest to foreign tourists who come to admire the Neo-Doric mausoleum built by Giuseppe Barbieri in 1828. It is a square plan with an internal corridor and an external colonnade. The side which faces the city, that is, the entrance is slightly raised and hence stands out from the rest of the building. Two sculpted lions

The Monumental Cemetery was the work of Giuseppe Barbieri.

(carved by Pegrassi using Canova's models) guard the entrance. The facade is in the form of an open vestibule with three aisles, with Doric columns crowned by a metope frieze and freely-inspired triglyphs. At the top the angel sounds the trumpet, announcing the resurrection, and below the word "resurrecturis" is inscribed. Apart from a little brick decoration, the facade is constructed in tufa. Inside there are a few finely sculpted funereal monuments of interest. The nearby gardens accommodate the ruins of an ancient temple dedicated to Jupiter, moved here in 1926 from via Armando Diaz (see Itinerary I). Retracing one's steps and continuing on along via Pallone, one arrives at BRA' SQUARE. This large square, full of light and the architectural colour of almost every epoch, includes the Arena.

In the Medieval period , this area was called the "braida" (from "breit" meaning "wide open space"). Antonio Borghi's 1878 monument to King Vittorio Emanuele II (the King on horseback) stands out in the middle. Also there, is the Monument to the Partisans by Mario Salazzari, and right in the centre, surrounded by a lovely garden, the Fountain of the Alps

The clock on the gate to the Brà has witnessed ups and downs, at times, ludicrous. Already in 1584 the idea of placing a clock on the ancient gates had been mentioned but then forgotten. This would give the people the time. The idea was reproposed in 1797 by the Patriotic Society which wanted to take the clock from Campo Marzio and place it in the Brà. But nothing came of this project either in 1809 or in 1812 notwithstanding the number of ideas which came forward, including the use of the bell mechanism of the Gardello Tower. The fall of the Italian Government and the Austrian occupation (in 1814) delayed the scheme yet again. Another futile attempt was made in 1853. Finally, on 2 June, 1972, after lengthy works the clock one admires today (and which was donated to the city by Count Antonio Nogarola) was put in place. However, initially it did not function well, being always either late or early. The Veronese, evidently bothered by this, took to referring sarcastically to the generous donation as "No gà l'ora" (Nogarola) meaning "time not given!".

The gates to the Brà at the end of the big avenue corso Porta Nuova lead into Brà Square.

(1975) - symbolising the twinning of Verona and the Bavarian city of Munich. The Arena is not the only important building which looks out onto the square. Where the wide avenue (corso Porta Nuova) finishes, the majestic gates to the Brà rise up, with the adjoining pentagonal tower. This is the entrance for those who approach Verona from the south. These two stone arches (1480) were set into the wall before the alterations ordered by Visconti. The left side of the square - for those approaching from the avenue - hosts the PHILHARMONIC ACADEMY and the MAFFEI EPIGRAPHIC MUSEUM. The former, founded in 1543, includes a museum - library with one literary and two musical foundations, as well as a collection of Renaissance wind instruments. The strong arm of the Academy has always been the Philharmonic Theatre where even young Mozart performed in 1770. Its construction (in 1605) was a modification - by Domenico Curtoni - of Palladio's design. Later the building was reconstructed (1716-1729) using a design by Francesco Bibiena. Partially destroyed by fire in 1749 and bombed in 1945, its present

The Maffei Epigraphic Museum contains a vast number of ancient, valuable documents.

reconstruction dates back to 1969. The Doric cloister by Alessandro Pompei was added onto the Ionic open vestibule in the first half of the 18 C. It was later appropriated by Scippione Maffei to house the 16 C. lapidary collection belonging to Nichesola, which had then been enlarged over the centuries. This building was subjected to various alterations until it took its definitive form when restored by Arrigo Rudi. Rudi also reordered the collection which is mainly milestones; busts; many Greek tablets; and Etruscan, Roman, Christian and Medieval tablets with inscriptions and illustrations of all kinds. Then one crosses over at the bottom of via Roma to the LISTON - favourite (and fashionable) promenade area for the Veronese. It is an 18 C. broad pavement situated along the north-west side of the Brà and lined with palaces and porticoes. Worth noting are the OTTOLINI PALACE at number 26; the 15 C. GUGLIENZI PALACE at number 20 (it also has 18 C. features and Francesco Morone's fresco of a "Madonna and Child" on the facade); the 16 C. RIGHETTINI PALACE at number 18, followed by the MALFATTI (ex-

Guastaverza) PALACE. Designed by
Sanmicheli, the Malfatti Palace was
one of the first meeting places in the
square and was where Silvia
Curtoni Verza hosted her famous
salons. The FACCIOLI HOME at
number 10 was designed by Luigi
Trezza, built in 1790. The
CAMPAGNA PALACE at number 2,
in Classical style, has been the
home of the Literary Society for
almost two hundred years. Behind
the Liston, in via Carlo Cattaneo, is
the Gothic-style DA LISCA HOME -
built C. 1450, but it has a beautiful
Renaissance portal. Next door is a
house which was built in 1506.
Five streets converge at the end of
the Liston: via Carlo Cattaneo, via
Oberdan, via Alberto Mario, via
Dietro Anfiteatro and the renowned
via Mazzini (which is amply dealt
with in Itinerary 2).
The north-east side of the square is
occupied entirely by the Roman
Amphitheatre, better known as the
ARENA. This imposing structure
was probably built about 100 A.D.
The architects of the masterpiece

are unknown but it was usual, in
that time, for public works of this
kind to be built by national
construction companies which were
specialized in the field and helped
by tradesmen recruited in the area.
Verona's amphitheatre is a
construction which was typical of
the Roman culture and it is the third
largest in existence, preceded by the
Colosseum in Rome and the
amphitheatre in Capua.
Structurally, it has been well-
preserved. It was built using, above
all, the stone extracted from the
quarries at Sant'Ambrogio di
Valpolicella - a town about 20 km
from Verona.
The elliptical flat area's internal
axes measure 73 m. by 44 m while
the external axes measure 152 m x
123 m, boundary wall included. The
circumference of the present
boundary is 391 metres.
Unfortunately, only one wing of the
external ring of arches whose
function was principally to adorn,
has survived (the Wing- which has
assumed mythical proportions).

*The Liston - a
fashionable
promenade which
extends beyond the
porticoes of the old
palaces.*

Entirely constructed in stone, it is a formation of three tiers of arches and it reached the awesome height of 30 m with a circumference of 435 m. Each tier counted 72 arches which were supported by 73 enormous pillars made of squared blocks of stone. The mighty external upper ring collapsed when a big earthquake shook the city in the 12 C. The middle ring which nowadays forms the facade of the amphitheatre is made up of two tiers: each has 72 arches and each is 18 m high. The flights of steps on the inside, both single and double, were constructed later. The second ring is linked to the third which, in turn, is linked to the fourth by a barrel vault which forms an internal tunnel 9 m high and about 4 m wide. From here, by ascending a few steps which lead into openings historically known as the "vomitories", one arrives at the terraces of the horseshoe-shaped auditorium which were reconstructed during the time of the Venetian Republic (1405-1801). Originally this area was broken up into rings, each having a separate entrance.The first, called the "podium" was set aside for the authorities and distinguished visitors. Another three rings and an upper gallery completed the horseshoe-shaped auditorium whose terraces in Verona marble are, on average 40 cm high and about 70 cm deep. In all there are 44 terraces. The Arena was constructed about 80 m beyond the city wall, but when towards 265 A. D. King Gallieno was forced to reinforce Verona's defence structures urgently, he had the original wall extended to include the amphitheatre. The Arena can hold about 22,000 people (seated) but on some occasions this number has been amply exceeded. Having cited the historical-technical data of the monument, let us now briefly mention the spectacles which have been hosted here over the last two thousand years. Ancient evidence reveals that in Roman times fights between ferocious beats from Africa took place, as did gladiator fights. A memorial tablet conserved at the Maffei Epigraphic Museum records the twenty-seven heroic duels fought by a certain Generoso; yet there is no documentation of the execution of the early Christians. In the late Middle Ages the amphitheatre began to lose, in part, its designation as a venue for spectacles. The 12 C. saw the beginning of sessions called "The Judgment of God": duels fought by cavaliers specially chosen by the contending parties. Recorded also are duels fought on judicial grounds between rival - even neighbouring - cities and the carrying out of capital punishment. The date 13 February, 1278 stands out as a tragic day for it witnessed the burning of 166 heretics. In those dark years the arched chambers under the tiers provided a home for the city's prostitutes and there they remained until the end of the 15 C. From the Middle Ages until the middle of the 18 C even tournaments and fairs are recorded as having taken place in the chivalrous tradition of the epoch. From 1600 onwards, apart from races and spectacles of all kinds, there were also bullfights. These were very popular and were known as "the hunting of the bull". They consisted of a kind of bullfight where the part of the toreador was played by a big dog, usually a mastiff specially trained in fighting bulls, and in turn, incited by teasing and red cloth put in front of him by real toreadors. When the dog won, his owner received a prize. There were always crowds of spectators, even foreigners and famous people. Two stone tablets record the presence of Emperor Jozef II in 1769 and

Facing page, above: the Wing of the Arena is all that remains of the original external ring which was made up of three tiers of arches; Below: the Arena rises up majestically in Brà Square, surrounded by other important monuments which include the Municipal Chambers and the Fountain of the Alps.

Napoleon Bonaparte in 1805. Still in the 18 C., the recitation of comedy began to take root. Performances took place during the summer months and in daylight using a wooden theatre set. This practice remained for many years. At the beginning of the 20 C. the Arena still hosted spectacles of all kinds - until the dawn of what can be called the "cultural revolt". This began in 1913 when the then-famous tenor from Verona, Giovanni Zenatello and some of his friends, had the idea of staging "Aida" in the Arena. Little did they realise what they had started, for after the "consecration" of the 1913 season, the annual opera season quickly became an international institution. Ever since that initial season - with the exception of two breaks due to war - millions of spectators have packed into the pinkish terraces of the two-thousand-year-old amphitheatre each summer. Behind the Arena one can see what remains of Gallieno's wall: later

added onto the original city boundary wall, while the east side of the Brà is dominated by the large Neo-Classical CITY COUNCIL CHAMBERS, built between 1835-48 on the design of the architect, Giuseppe Barbieri. A majestic building of the Corinthian order with a colonnade and open vestibule, it is approached by a very wide staircase. Made up of a central section with two wings it is reminiscent of Palladio. A semi-circular construction has recently been added on at the back. The Reception Lounge is decorated with three large canvases: by Paolo Farinati ("Battle of the Veronese against Barbarossa at Vigasio" - a small town near Verona); by Felice Brusasorzi ("Victory of the Veronese at Salò in 1849") and by Benedetto and Carletto Caliari ("Supper at the

A magical moment during one of the nocturnal performances in the Arena.

home of the Pharisee"). The south side has a monumental palace, that of the GREAT GUARD (Gran Guardia), and home to many cultural manifestations. It is a continuation of the battlemented city wall and marks the northernmost point of the "cittadella" (city fortress), hence the adjoining watch tower. Started in 1610 but only finished in 1836 by Giuseppe Barbieri and Enrico Storari, its lower floor in ashlar is characterized by a series of arches which together form a lower portico. This stylistic feature is reflected in the shape of the five large central windows on the floor above. The construction of very long rows of steps leading up to the building proved to be the solution to the difference in level between the palace and the square.

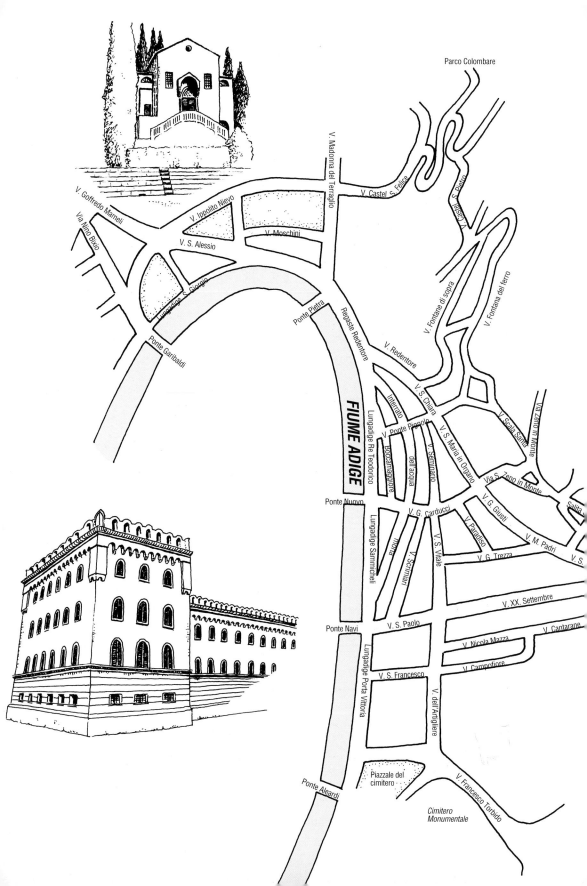

Parco Colombare

V. Madonna del Terraglio

V. Castel S. Felice

V. Castel S. Pietro

V. Goffredo Mameli

V. Ippolito Nievo

V. Moschini

V. S. Alessio

Via Nino Bixio

Lungadige S. Giorgio

Ponte Pietra

Ponte Garibaldi

Regaste Redentore

V. Redentore

V. Fontane di sopra

V. Fontana del ferro

FIUME ADIGE

Interrato

V. S. Chiara

V. Ponte Pignolo

Boccamaggiore

dell'acqua

V. Seminario

V. S. Maria in Organo

V. Scala Santa

Via S. Zeno in Monte

Salita

Lungadige Re Teodorico

Ponte Nuovo

V. G. Carducci

V. G. Giusti

V. Zeno in Monte

Lungadige Sammicheli

Interra

V. Scrimari

V. S. Vitale

V. Paradiso

V. M. Padri

V. S.

V. G. Trezza

Ponte Navi

V. XX. Settembre

V. S. Paolo

V. Nicola Mazza

V. Cantarane

Lungadige Porta Vittoria

V. S. Francesco

V. Campofiore

V. dell'Artigliere

Ponte Aleardi

Piazzale del cimitero

V. Francesco Torbido

Cimitero Monumentale

FROM ST. GEORGE'S GATE TO NEW VICTORY GATE

St. George's Gate - Church of St. George in the Open
(in Braida) - St. Stephen's Church - St. Peter's Castle
- Roman Theatre - Church of St. John in the Valley
- Church of St. Mary in the Organ - Organ Gate
- Church of St. Thomas of Canterbury (Cantuariense)
- Giusti Gardens - Church of Sts. Nazaro and Celso
- St. Toscana's Church - University of Verona
- Natural History Museum - New Victory Gate

*This is an itinerary which explores important moments in
the history of Veronetta: the area which spreads between the
left bank of the Adige and the hills which overlook it. This
zone developed after the Treaty of Luneville (1801) which
divided the city in two, assigning the left bank to the
Austrians and the right bank to the French.
The route described here is shorter than the other four but
important, for it is strongly characterized by the course of
the river which, in some places, flows beside the hills on
which Verona extends its northeastern suburbs. The route
begins at the edge of the modern residential suburb of Borgo
Trento and finishes at the New Victory Gate (Ponte della
Vittoria Nuova). The square outside the Church of St. George
in Braida (in the open) or Isolo Square are recommended
carparks.*

St. George's Gate is named after the nearby Church of St. George in Braida.

At the northern edge of the old city one arrives at ST. GEORGE'S GATE which is also known as Trento Gate. (The road leads north to Trento). Built by Sanmicheli in 1525, it is of modest dimensions with a facade in white stone scanned by four Doric pillars. The part facing inwards towards the city is in tufa and was added on by the Austrians in 1838. The rampants which were once attached are visible even today.

A little further on, the CHURCH OF ST. GEORGE IN BRAIDA (from "breit" meaning "wide open") with its unmistakle Sanmichelian dome and its unfinished bell-tower is almost mirrored in the Adige. The origins of the church are unclear, much documentation having been lost during the Middle Ages. There is a document which confirms the existence of a church dedicated to St. George as early as 780. A Benedictine monastery was founded here in 1006 and restored in 1127 after the big earthquake of 1117. In1442 the monastery was entrusted to the Canons of St. George in Alga of Venice and in 1477 they rebuilt the temple in the form we admire today.

The white marble facade with two lines of Ionic and Corinthian pillars houses the statues of Sts. George and Lawrence Giustiniani in two side niches. The rest of the building is in brick. The stupendous dome by Sanmicheli highlights the church as does the "squashed" bell-tower (albeit, negatively) realised by Brugnoli on the design, not adhered to, of Sanmicheli.

The interior has one central nave which is simple yet grand. The windows which open on the drum of the dome give plenty of light and exalt the chromatism. This church houses many artistic masterpieces, especially along the left side. Above the main door one can see Tintoretto's large canvas "The Baptism of Christ" (unfortunately, poorly lit), while at ground level there are two elegant 16 C. holy water fonts. The first chapel on the left houses Francesco Caroto's altarpiece of "St. Ursula with the Virgin" (1545) while the second chapel has De Stefani's "Martyrdom of St. Lawrence" (1564). Of great artistic value is Francesco Caroto's tryptych (1551) "Sts. Rocco and Sebastian" in the third chapel. This tryptych frames Recchia's "St. Joseph with Child" (1882) while above there is an oval by Brusasorzi and even further up a "Tranfiguration" by F. Caroto. The fourth chapel is dedicated to Sts. Lawrence, Zeno and Sylvester and houses a "Madonna of the Boundary with Sts. Lawrence and Zeno" by Girolamo dai Libri, perhaps the highest placed masterpiece in the church. To note, in particular, is the choir of angels below the Virgin's throne. Then follows the Baptistry with Bernardino India's "Two Soldiers, Martyrs" (1571) flanking Moretto da Brescia's "St. Cecilia and the Holy Martyrs" (1540) which is placed under the organ. Just before the presbytery is an "Annunciation" by Giovanni Caroto, followed by the majestic high altar with "The Martyrdom of St. George" - Paolo Veronese's masterpiece, 1565-66. There are two enormous canvases on the sides: one by Farinati ("Multiplication of the Loaves and Fishes") and the other by Felice Brusasorzi ("Madonna of the Desert").

The right wall is decidedly less significant in artistic value. The first altar has a "Noli me tangere" by Montemezzano (1578), while the second boasts an "Assumption and Saint" by Ottino (1625). The third is characterized by a 1619 canvas of the "Descent of the Holy Spirit" by Domenico Robusti (Tintoretto's son), and the fourth has a canvas of the "Virgin, Archangels and

A spectacular nocturnal view of the Church of St. George in Braida with its lights reflecting in the Adige.

Above: "Madonna and Saints" - a detail of the painting by Girolamo dai Libri.

To the right: "Saint Cecilia and the Holy Martyrs" by Moretto da Brescia. Both paintings are conserved in the Church of St. George in Braida.

Once the land here was a favourite haunt of painters who often stopped to paint pictures of lanes and the facades of houses which were dotted along the riverbank. Angelo Dall'Oca Bianca, in particular, loved depicting these places which lived in symbiosis with the river. The construction of new embarkments after the floods of 1882 dramatically changed the appearance of the zone, but one can still gather the threads of a pulsing popular character in the houses which face the Lungadige San Giorgio along to the CHURCH OF ST. PETER, THE MARTYR (1656). The little streets at the back hide, as do the deconsecrated Churches of St. Alessio, St. Ursula of the Mendicants and Our Lady of the Lily. Gothic balconies jut out above Renaissance porches here and there. Vicolo Verza (a lane), masterfully represented by Agostino Bonetti, embodies in just a few metres, the spirit of this quarter.

ST. STEPHEN'S CHURCH is almost opposite the stone bridge. The ancient place of worship was built on the basilica plan, as testified by the long windows on the sides, closed in or later reduced in size to

Tobiolo" by Felice Brusasorzi (1582). Under the choir, facing the organ is the "Miracle of St. Barnabas" - a copy of Veronese's masterpiece which hangs in the Museum of Rouen - and it is flanked by two gigantic "Sts. Jerome and Gregory" by Bernardino India.

The "Judgment of St. George" by Romanino (1540) has been divided and placed at the sides of the choir. The structure is completed by the rectangular cloister which faces the Adige. The walk along the Adige which meanders round to the stone bridge (ponte della Pietra) is extremely panoramic and relaxing.

An extremely old vegetable garden at the back of ST. GEORGE'S MONASTERY was perhaps the site of the massacre of 11,000 Paduans perpetrated by Ezzelino da Romano in 1256. Rolandino records that the extermination was effected by famine, thirst, the cold, use of the pitchfork or spade and fire. Although various evidence of this horrible event exists, many doubts still remain about the spot where the deed is said to have taken place especially about the number put to death. The death toll appears to be exaggerated if one considers that at that time the population of the entire city of Padua was only 15,000.

fit the Romanesque style. In fact, it could be presumed that this was the cathedral until the 8 C. Evidence of this is provided by the primitive stone (episcopal) chair which is conserved in the apse and the numerous tombs of Veronese Bishops found here.

The Church has been rebuilt and restored over the centuries but it can be said that the outer walls, at least in part, are those of the original 4-5 C church. Its actual appearance is attributed to 12 C. except for the apse which was renovated towards the early 14 C. The facade is simple: tufa and brick with a small gabled arch which overhangs the red marble portal. The central rose window and the two side windows were 19 C. additions. Original, though, is the octagonal, brick bell-tower. The interior is a Latin cross with a nave and two side aisles. The church has an upper level, a lower level and a crypt. A large altarpiece by Brusasorzi hangs above the portal. Then, on the right after a fresco by Miolato, is the Chapel of the Holy Innocents frescoed by Pasquale Ottino, with, on the left wall, a painting by Orbetto ("Martyrdom of the Forty") and on the right "Five Bishops" by Bassetti. According to tradition, this chapel - which is a glittering example of Veronese Baroque - custodies the relics of four children killed in the slaughter ordered by Herod. Their remains were brought up from the crypt. Furthermore, this chapel also keeps the mortal remains of forty Veronese martyrs and five bishop-saints.

The altarpiece of the last altar in the opposite aisle is worth noting: "St. Stephen" by Dal Moro who is also responsible for the painting of the same saint in the lunette above the side door. Two large monochromatic frescoes, one on the right wall and the other on the left, depict St. Stephen's ordination as a deacon and later, his burial. Very old paintings of unknown authorship appear here and there on the walls.

A wide loop of the Adige coincides with the position of St. George's Church and creates a lovely walk.

The facade of the ancient St. Stephen's Church.

After ascending the steps which lead to the presbytery, one sees the 14 C statue in tufa of St. Peter. The work of Rigino d'Enrico, it came from the Church of St. Peter on the Hill when it was demolished and was, undoubtedly, one of the most valuable pieces. Also to be admired are the splendidly restored "Annunciation" by Martino da Verona and a "Coronation of the Virgin". The fully decorated dome was the work of Brusasorzi while the altar at the back, on the right of the cross vault, houses Francesco Caroto's "Madonna and Sts. Peter and Paul".

The crypt is interesting, with its four arches - probably 8 C. - and its contents: plunder from the Roman epoch and early Middle Ages. Not to be forgotten, either, is an "Annunciation" by Sartori and a statue of St. Stephen by dell'Aglio. However, the moment of greatest impact comes when one sees the remains of a small nave - perhaps 8 C - with even older columns and capitals. This indicates just how complex the history of this church is. Outside, once more, behind the apse, one walks uphill slightly, past the Teatro laboratorio (Theatre Workshop) and turns right up VIA SAN CARLO, where the church of the same name forms part of the Mazza College complex.

Continuing on up, one reaches the Maximilian wall which unites St. Felix and St. Peter's Castles. The latter affords a wonderful panorama of the city and it can be reached by driving up the road which winds around the hill. But much more enchanting (albeit, tiring) is the walk up the steps which begins down by the river at the beginning of the Regaste Redentore, almost beside the Roman Theatre.

The area which surrounds ST. PETER'S CASTLE could be called the reliquary of Veronese civilisation. It was the first site of the Rhaetian-Euganee people who established a colony on this hill.

The Roman acropolis probably sprang up here. We know that the cemetery of the Church of St. John in the Valley was located on the hillside. It was also the first place of Christian worship which imposed itself on paganism. Theodoric established his court here and projected fortifications, which were successively reinforced by the Lombards and Franks.

When the Austrians razed the Castle ruins to the ground in 1840 to build the monumental barracks, they also demolished the Romanesque Church of St. Peter at the Castle, along with its origins. During excavations numerous artefacts came to the surface - prehistoric objects and Roman sculpture - but all these have, unfortunately, been lost thereby rendering it impossible to study, in depth, the vicissitudes of this important site and to be able to understand, above all, the configuration of the hill under Roman rule.

Not far from here is the small Romanesque CHURCH OF NAZARETH - until the 1 C., a place of retreat for the city's bishops. It has a 15 C. apse but the architecture of the main door is 14 C. Sante Creara's "Christ being taken down from the Cross" is conserved inside.

Returning to Lungadige Terraglio, a small 16 C. palace acts as entrance to the Roman Theatre and to an archaeological zone which extends down the southern slopes of the hillside from St. Peter's Castle. Built at the foot of the hill in the last quarter of 1 A.D., the ROMAN THEATRE is an edifice which was typical of the Greek culture both in terms of structure and construction techniques. Together with the Roman Theatre in Trieste, it is the most intersting of those in the Tri-Veneto both in terms of size and state of preservation. A semi-circle in the form of an inverted cone dug out of a rock on the hill, supports

The Chapel of the Holy Innocents frescoed by Pasquale Ottino, in St. Stephen's Church.

The short rather steep climb up to St. Peter's Castle is a joyous walk up the hill past the ancient houses dotted among the greenery, Roman ruins, evidence of the Middle Ages with views which continue to open out as one goes higher. Ponte Pietra (Stone Bridge), the Roman Theatre, the perfect loop of the river which winds around the foot of the hill (the first high ground of the Veronese prealps), the Church of St. George in Braida all appear and disappear below as one moves around corners; the walk culminating in a vast and splendid panorama at the top. And here, apart from the view, one also admires the imposing barracks built by the Austrians. On the left there is a Medieval wall mounted with merlons while, all around, the odd villa tries to peer through the olive trees. The summit is obviously the favourite meeting place for those in love or simply for those wanting a quiet spot in which to reflect. The view at night is particularly evocative with the city below lit up while, in the distance, the yellow lights of the motorway mark the boundary between city and plain.

the so-called terraces. In Roman times the stage was located facing the terraces with the Adige flowing by behind, and the space in front was for the orchestra (nowadays it is the stalls area).

The stage has been partially preserved. It was originally divided into three parts: the centre, which was deep and curved, with two wings which were smaller and rectangular in shape. The lower part of the horseshoe-shaped auditorium (ima cavea), made of wide steps of white stone was divided into six sections in the form of wedges. The upper part (summa cavea) has not been reconstructed but it was thought to have consisted of twelve wide steps. Tufa, being somewhat perishable, was used for the less exposed parts of the construction.

A semicircular walkway which was two metres high overhung the terraces: over one-third still exists. There is also a gallery at the top,

The Roman Theatre - a view of the horseshoe-shaped auditorium and the surrounding architecture.

decorated with small arches which have the names of the most important Veronese families engraved on them.

The construction has undergone enormous damage due to earthquakes, floods and war over the centuries, but continues to endure and be used.

In the same area a high wall was constructed. The purpose of this was to separate the MONASTERY OF ST. JEROME (Girolamo) and the CHURCH OF STS. SIRO AND LIBERA above, from the Roman Theatre, below.

During the Middle Ages the theatre became a haven for hermits and artists who came to pray and work. In the 16 C., with the flowering of the Renaissance, it offered inspiration for pictures depicting ideal reconstructions. Giovanni Caroto and Andrea Palladio were part of this group artists. At the end of the 19 C., the whole zone was taken over by the City Council who

St. Siro's Church looks out over one side of the ancient Roman Theatre.

St. Peter's hill got its name from a church built at the top towards the end of the 4 C. The church was restored in 811 through the efforts of Archdeacon Pacifico and later gained the attention of King Berengar I who, from 890 onwards, used to go there at about midnight to take part in religious ceremonies.

After some time a few enemies came to know of this habit and one night they organized an ambush: taking advantage of the dark they surrounded the church in March 924. When Berengar arrived at the top of the path on time and unescorted, as usual, the conspirators came out from the shadows and murdered him. The King's blood mixed with the mud and stained a big stone which stood in front of the church. On discovering the crime the following day, the body was recomposed and orders were given to clear up the area, but it proved to be impossible to clean the stone.

Berengar's body was buried on the spot where he died and he was immediately honoured as a saint. In 1607 a soldier - like Barbarian woman violated the tomb and strew the bones all over the hill. Story has it, however, that even at the beginning of the 19 C. it was still possible to see his presumed tomb at the top of the hill.

began a restoration project which, after various setbacks, was finally completed in 1959.

Inside the area occupied by the Theatre, just above the terraces, one is aware of the facade of the CHURCH OF ST. SIRO AND LIBERA.

Built at the beginning of the 10 C. in honour of St. Siro, its dedication was later broadened to include Saint Libera (14 C.).

Elegant sets of steps with two branches (constructed 1697-1705) give access to the church whose entrance has an overhanging 14 C. Gothic gabled arch. On the lower arch (the rise) above the main door, is a "Christ with St. John, the Baptist and Mary Magdalen" (1366).

The upper lunette shows "St. Siro on the bishop's chair betwen Sts. Libera and Faustina crowned", and the lower, a "Madonna with Child between two saints". On the inside, the wooden chair carved by Andrea Kraft and Rodolfo Sint (1717-20) and the tomb of the painter, Giambettino Cignaroli are worth noting.

By crossing the stalls of the theatre and climbing up to the last bank of steps, one arrives at a small loggia from which it is possible to take a lift which goes to ST. JEROME'S

MONASTERY, home of the ARCHAEOLOGICAL MUSEUM which Antonio Avena founded in 1924. It houses an important collection of Roman, Greek and Etruscan artefacts.

In the Mosaics Room a gladiator Fight (1 A.D.), a sculpture of a prince's head which belonged to the Giulia Claudia family (1 A.D.) and a loricate bust of the same epoch deserve attention. Greek and Italian ceramics are on display in the reliquaries. The cells which follow exhibit coloured glass, bronzes and sculptures which also line the corridor and there is a Roman copy of a Menander. The refectory is lined with urns, mosaics, funereal stems and sculptures, including a valuable "female figure seated". The cloister and courtyard contain Roman-Veronese artefacts and funereal monuments.

The church has an early-Christian flooring (recovered from St. Stephen's) and Francesco Caroto's triumphal arch with a fresco of the "Annunciation" (1508). The altar has a Renaissance tryptich. Then there is a second cloister where one can see fragments of funereal monuments, and a double-faced

Below left: the steep steps which lead up to St. Peter's Castle.

Below right: the refined facade of the Sagromoso Palace.

herma (2 C.) There is a hollow space in the tufa. It was probably excavated at one time to protect the theatre below from infiltration of water.

After leaving the Roman Theatre proceed left along via Redentore and then veer left into via Santa Chiara (St. Clare) where the 16 C. SAGRAMOSO PALACE, a classical construction decorated by a frieze by Dal Moro, stands.

In Borgo Tascheria, instead, there is a 13 C. house in tufa worth seeing. Closed in by a gate, in a small recess, is ST. CLARE'S CHURCH (1424) with a brick facade and Gothic-arched door which depicts, in the lunette, "ST. CLARE PROTECTING HER NUNS, THE POOR CLARES". The facade is completed by two three-lobed side windows and a central Gothic window.

Internally it has one nave and conserves two Renaissance altars, one of which is embellished by frescoes of the "Evangelists", "God the Father", and "Two Prophets" (by Michele da Verona and Francesco Morone) while the chapel opposite is adorned with candelabra (attributed to Domenico da Lugo).

Just before arriving at St. Clare's Church there is a street on the left called via SAN GIOVANNI IN VALLE along which, by climbing up a small distance, one arrives at the church of the same name. The church was built on top of the ruins of firstly, a pagan necropolis and then, a Christian cemetery. It took on its present appearance in the first half of the 12 C. The facade is in tufa and has a fine, small, gabled arch which frames a "Madonna with Child and saints" of unknown authorship (perhaps Stefano da Zevio or Altichiero).

The sides reveal a very simple structure while the three apses are embellished at the top with framed arches, semi-columns and

Corinthian capitals. The bell-tower was completed in the 16 C but its lower part is Romanesque in style. The cloister has been able to regain its original graceful form (after the transformation to which it was subjected during the 18 C.) thanks to careful restoration work effected this century. The rectory is a rare construction and, like the church, can be dated c. 1120.

Inside, the church has a nave and two aisles which are divided by alternating pillars and columns. Typically Romanesque in style, it is made up of one section called the PLEBANA and the presbytery. The walls are covered with fragments of frescoes of unknown authorship and there is an elaborate 18 C., Baroque altar in red and white marble, with a sculpture of St. John, the Baptist on the altar-rail.

The crypt has three small naves with various columns and capitals

The Church of St. John in the Valley.

and conserves a faded "Adoration of the Magi" on the right of the high altar and a "Madonna on the throne" on the left - both of the school of Altichiero. The side apse on the right has a rich, 14 C decoration of rosettes and rhombi. On the high altar, the Renaissance tabernacle stands out and on the sides, two finely-sculpted, red marble sarcophagi are to be admired. The urn on the left, said to be of pagan origin, belongs to the 3 C.

The mortal remains of Sts. Simon and Jude were found under the main altar. That they were them seems to be an unquestionable fact since, on this site, there was a pre-existent Christian cemetery.

Before leaving this church which is full of history, religious faith and tradition, let us take a quick look at the only external votive niche. It is supported by a capital (probably 12 C.) and made up of a small base held up by four small columns which enclose a sculpture of St. John, the Baptist, unfortunately in a sad state of repair.

A number of small streets branch off from St. John in the Valley. One of these, via Fontana del Ferro leads one quickly to VILLA FRANCESCATTI (1845), nowadays the youth hostel. The park, which is adorned with grottoes, is worth a visit.

Continuing on, towards the hill,

The bas-relief of "St. Clare protecting her nuns, the Poor Clares" located on the door of St. Clare's Church.

one arrives at the spot where the Fountain del Fèro sprang up. This ancient fountain was once a place of pilgrimage for those in love, especially on the feast of St. John, the Baptist.

Back at St. John's Church, one sees a Ducal court on the right: a nucleus of buildings dating back to the early Middle Ages which enclose two courtyards while vicolo Pozza leads one to the AFRICAN MUSEUM OF THE COMBONI MISSIONARIES which illustrates and amply documents the culture and tradition of various African races.

By other streets, one can also reach the CHURCH OF ST. ZENO ON THE MOUNT (ex Our lady of Bethlehem, an enormous, imposing structure which is the Institute of Charity of Don Calabria, and is dominated by a gigantic cross visible at a great distance.

Returning to the river once more one arrives in Interrato dell'Acqua Morta (meaning Silted up with dead water) which got its rather strange name from the operations carried out to dry up this arm of the Adige after the floods of 1882. Beforehand, an arm passed by here thereby creating a small island, known as the Isolo. Reclamation of the land here not only obliterated, forever, the Middle Ages character of this quarter but also swept away all the river activity (trade, transport, mills, markets and pubs). Isolo was always very attached to the CHURCH OF ST. MARY IN THE ORGAN situated at the Pignolo Bridge - a point where the constant coming and going of the people created a colourful comic choreography.

St. Mary in the Organ dates back to the 6 C. It was rebuilt after the 1117 earthquake and then in 1444 it passed into the hands of the White Benedictines (better known as the Olivetans). It was they who

restructured the church as we see it today. Rich in masterpieces, it has, however, been subjected to the ups and downs of history, in particular, the arrival of Napoleon Bonaparte who stripped the church of most of its precious works including a number of altars with wood inlay (the work of Frà Giovanni of Verona).

The unfinished facade bears witness to a composite style: Gothic-Romanesque on the upper part while the lower part, in the style of Sanmicheli, was inspired by the Malatestas of Rimini and characterized by a grand central arch flanked by two side arches, the whole completed by four columns with friezes.

The elegant Renaissance bell-tower, designed by Frà Giovanni, was the work of Francesco Lapicida (c. 1533). The restructured cloister is, nowadays, a nursery school.

The Gothic-Romanesque interior is in the form of a Latin cross. The lower church has a nave and two aisles and the upper church was built above a pre-existent church. The powerful Baroque organ is above the main entrance; on the right is a canvas by Savoldo and on the left, a canvas by Pittoni. The central vault has been repainted, brightening Francesco Cannella's original of 1790.

A sequence of frescoes on the pediments of the nave deserve a mention: those on the right are by Francesco Caroto, those on the left, by Nicolò Giolfino.

The first chapel on the right, dedicated to St. Anthony, shows off Antonio Balestra's alterpiece. The second and third contain no notable works, while the fourth houses an altarpieces depicting "St. Michael, the Archangel" by Farinati and two frescoes of Saints on the sides. Giordano Mocetto's "Virgin on the Throne with Sts. Stephen and Catherine" hangs above the confessional, Then follows the spacious chapel dedicated to St. Francis of Rome with Guercino's altarpiece. Externally, there are interesting frescoes by Torbido (two saints, below) and Cavazzola (the archangels, above). Right of the high altar is the Chapel of the Holy Cross and St. Helen with frescoes by Giolfino. Simone Brentana painted the altarpiece while externally, the valuable "Ascension" (above) is the work of Giolfino and an equally admirable "Annunciation" (below) is the work of Cavazzola.

Facing page, above: the interior of the Church of St. Mary in the Organ.

Below: the facade.

While walking round Verona one often notes engravings on walls or houses which indicate the level the Adige has arrived at when in flood over the years. One date is recurrent: September, 1882.

The disaster was of such magnitude that it changed the course of history of Verona forever.

The Adige broke its banks during the night of the 15th and 16th September while the rain was pelting down (as it had done for days) and the vibrations and force of the waters was so strong that the windows of the houses in the vicinity shattered. Survivors recounted that there was a roar and then the waters surged through the centre of the city, filling cellars and basements, alleyways, lanes, squares and streets, and the low lying areas of the city were subject to frightening whirlpools. At dawn of the 17th September what people saw was an apocalypse for where streets had been, torrents flowed, squares were transformed into pools; in fact, more than two-thirds of Verona and its immediate periphery was flooded out. At 2 p.m. that day the river was 4.5 metres higher than its safety mark. Even the boats in service along corso Porta dei Borsari were unable to pass under the arches to enter the street! Those who were courageous enough went down to the stone bridge to measure the depth of the river which resulted to be more than 12 metres while the average velocity was 20 km per hour - an enormous force if one considers that, over a distance of less than one kilometre the riverbed narrowed from 190m. at Giarina to 49 m. at St. Thomas' Church.

The damage was great. In the torrent one house in via Seghe was swept away drowning its 11 occupants. Rescue teams sought those who had taken refuge on the upper floors of their homes or on the roofs. Soldiers and firemen took turns in wading through the rush of the waters, going from house to house fastening ropes to chimneys and thereby creating a life-line. In so doing, they managed to save hundreds of lives.. However, at the same time, in Veronetta buildings collapsed: as a result of the violence of the current, their foundations gave way.

The final toll was that over half of Verona's buildings were flooded out up to the third-floor level. Of these about three hundred were completely destroyed or damaged beyond repair. Two bridges, also, were seriously affected while twenty of the biggest river mills which provided entire families of boatmen with work were swept away. This dealt a decisive blow to the city's river activities. The same fate awaited the twenty-seven water-scooping wheels used for the irrigation of the orchards in Campagnola, St. Zeno and other peripheral zones. Afterwards Verona was submerged in mud and silt, remained without lighting and had polluted water wells. The situation appeared so grave, in fact, that many people wondered if the city would survive. But the Veronese showed courage and set to work: the banks of the Adige were subsequently raised and strengthened, industry took off and the local newspaper (The New Arena) boldly spurred on the people with these words "The future is in our hands. Let us hold our heads high and work. May this be our motto".

The presbytery, especially the altar, underwent changes during the Baroque period. The central canvas depicts an "Assumption" by Giacinto Brandi while the side ones are by Paolo Farinati.

Pleasing, too, are Caroto's six landscapes which serve as a prelude to Frà Giovanni's choir of wood inlay. It is harmonious and exquisite in its most minute detail (1495-99). Also precious are the friar's walnut candelabra which are over 4 m. high, and the lectern.

But the real jewel of the church is the sacristy (1504) with its domed ceiling decorated with arabesques. It is lined with portraits of Benedictine Popes on one side and the most famous members of the order on the other. Francesco Morone's portrait of Frà Giovanni hangs above the small entrance which leads to the presbytery. Morone also painted the other frescoes.

Undoubtedly the high point, artistically speaking, is the back with its panels of carved and inlaid

To the right: Organ Gate.

New Testament Parables and Episodes (work of Cavazzola). Orbetto painted the altarpiece of "St. Anthony and Francis".
The 12 C crypt has a nave and two aisles. It is rich in spoils and various tombstones lie here and there.
Back in the upper church, left of the presbytery, is the impressive Chapel of Christ, the King which contains an altarpiece of "St. Benedict genuflecting" by Simone Brentana and frescoes by Brusasorzi.
The chapel dedicated to Blessed Bernardo Tolomei, founder of the Olivetan order, has a painting by Luca Giordano in the centre, as well as works by Giovanni Murari and Simone Brentana, not to mention the legendary "Little Mule". The Giusti Chapel hosts an altarpiece of the "Virgin on the Throne" by Francesco Morone.
The old 12 C. city wall which was once erroneously thought to have been part of Theodoric's fortifications, passes through this area near via Porta Organo. Having arrived at the barrel-vaulted, brick

wood - a masterpiece of the great friar, realized between 1519-1525. It rests on a large walnut bench whose doors have landscapes painted on them. The "Transfiguration" is, however, the work of Brusasorzi. The doors of the cupboards on the opposite side are decorated with

To the right: the facade of the Diocesan Seminary.

and tufa gate, one turns left into via Seminario where the DIOCESAN SEMINARY is located. This enormous edifice was begun by Ludovico Perini at the end of the 17 C. and completed by Ottone Calderari in the 18 C. Calderari added the Ionic-style atrium and the loggia which was later frescoed with the Signs of the Zodiac by Marco Marcola. The chapel contains "The Supper at Emmaus" by Coppa.

There are other interesting buildings in this street: the 15 C. Da Lisca Palace and elegant Veronese Renaissance mansions.

Around the corner, in via Carducci, one comes to the CHURCH OF ST. THOMAS OF CANTERBURY (Cantuariense), dedicated to the Bishop of Canterbury by the Carmelites. Begun in 1449 and consecrated in 1504, this majestic brick construction has, in effect, never been completed. Its portal (by Angelo di Giovanni, 1493) and Gothic windows are finely decorated, as is the beautiful central rose window. The bell-tower is in

the form of a pine-cone surrounded by four small pinnacles. The church has one central nave, and a trussed ceiling divided into three big arches.

Sanmicheli's sepulchral seal is located here. Eight Baroque altars line the sides: the first on the right custodies Sanmicheli's tomb (a 19 C work by Ugo Zannoni); other masterpieces are Orbetto's "Magdalena", Balestra's "Annunciation", Girolamo dai Libri's "Sts. Rocco, Sebastian and Job", Pomedello's "Climb up Calvary" (1524), Paolo Farinati's "Madonna appearing to Sts. Albert and Jerome", a "Sts. John the Baptist, Peter and Paul" (probably by Francesco Torbido) and a "Madonna in glory between Sts. Anthony Abbot and Onofrio" (1569) by Paolo Farinati.

There is a painted wooden Crucifix (probably 14 C.) in the right apse. Giuseppe Bonatti's huge Baroque organ is considered to be one of the finest organs in the city. Mozart performed on it when he was just 13. Back in via Carducci, proceed to

The internal facade of the Giusti Palace which is famous for its beautiful garden.

the intersection with via Giardini Giusti. On the left of Bernardi Square at number 41, one sees the GIUSTI PALACE and its gardens, built in the middle 16 C. The palace's facade was decorated by Orazio Farinati in 1591. The interior was frescoed by Francesco Lorenzi and Lodovico Dorigny. However, it is the GARDEN which is special: a quadrangle whose northern boundary is defined by the rocks of the surrounding hills, rendered enchanting by the solemn majesty of its trees, its fragrant box labyrinth (designed by Luigi Trezza at the end of the 18 C), the greenery and flowerbeds which cover the hill, the small paths dotted with statues and the mask with the balastraded terrace.

Facing page: interior of the Church of Saints Nazaro and Celso.

Beyond piazza Bernardi, continuing in a straight line up via Muro Padri to the end, one arrives at the CHURCH OF STS. NAZARO AND CELSO which was built on a pre-existent 8 C. chapel but adopted its present form at the end of the 15 C. Its history has been notable. The Edict of Napoleon in 1810, however, marked the beginning of its decline. Enclosed by a gate in a small square (the work of Saletti, 1688), the church stands out with its brick facade in Romanesque - Gothic style. The lunette above the portal reveals Paolo Ligozzi's beautifully-frescoed "Madonna and child". The square, 16 C. bell-tower is adorned with a clock - an element which is absent in the other bell-towers of Verona.

Internally, the church has one nave, two side aisles and three apses, scanned by pillars which support the vaulted arches. The second altar on the left houses a valuable painting by Antonio Badile, while the lunette depicts "The Temptations of St. Anthony" by Aliprandi. Note also Domenico Brusasorzi's "Madonna and Saints" at the fifth altar, followed by the

The young mule is a 13 C sculpture created in wood from the olive tree and then painted. It shows Christ blessing the crowd on his entry into Jerusalem. The statue has been the source of numerous legends, one of which mentions Christ's miraculous entry into the church through the Adige in flood. At the end of the 18 C. the original image was carried in procesion along all the adjacent alleyways of the church on Palm Sunday.

magnificent Chapel of St. Blaise. Built by Beltramo di Valsolda, in honour of the saint, between 1488-1508 it conserves his mortal remains in the raised altar-sarcophagus (work of Bernardino Panteo).

The Chapel contains a number of masterpieces: Falconetto and Domenico Morone's frescoed dome; a precious "Annunciation" by Cavazzola above the internal facade of the entrance arch; an altarpiece depicting the "Blessed Virgin in glory with Sts. Blaise, Sebastian and Juliana" and below, Girolamo dai Libri's "Miracle of St. Blaise", "Martyrdom of St. Sebastian and Martyrdom of St. Juliana". These works are crowned by Bartolomeo Montagna's frescoes which portray Episodes in the life of St. Blaise (from left: the saint in the desert; his arrest; his torture; his decapitation). There is a smaller chapel within this chapel dedicated to the Blessed Virgin of Pompei and St. Pius X. Here, albeit scarsely lit, one can admire three masterpieces by Palma, the younger: the "Nativity", "Circumcision" and "Presentation of Jesus at the Temple".

Left of this chapel is a small apse - the Britti Chapel - which contains G. Mocetto's "Blessed Virgin with

The external columns of the Church of Sts. Nazaro and Celso, distinct for their sculpted cloths.

and Montagna's paintings are worth noting. The high altar is modest, apart from a Venetian tabernacle dated 1537. In a niche above the door is a polychromatic statue (1400-1450) depicting a "Madonna on the Throne", of unknown authorship. The sacristy was well designed and its walls are embellished with two paintings by Montagna, one by Benaglio and one by Domenico Brusasorzi.

Along the right wall the altars host works by Giovanni Caliari and his famous son, Paolo (Veronese), Orlando Flacco, Dal Moro (fresco on the third altar), Farinati ("Annunciation" on the fourth altar) and Bernardino India's bold altarpiece, the "Conversion of St. Paul" on the fifth altar.

The choir is situated above the main entrance. Domenico Brusasorzi painted the doors of the organ console.

Outside again, at the intersection with via San Nazaro is the 16 C Bocca Trezza palace, restored in the 19 C. and the home of the state Institute of fine Arts "N. Nani". Inside, there are frescoes by Battista del Moro, Bernardino India, Paolo Farinati and Anselmo Canera. Continue up this road - stop to admire one of Torbido's frescoes - and just before arriving at porta Vescovo (Bishop's Gate) the extreme eastern boundary of the historic city, one enters a small square.

SAINT TOSCANA'S CHURCH - a tiny temple - stands on one side of this square. It is important for its representation of Verona's "minor" artworks and for the sense of peace which pervades: an oasis of peace in a zone where there is an intense flow of traffic.

Packed with history - testified by the composite styles of architecture and the different titles the church has had - it is preceded by a small courtyard enclosed which was once

Child on the throne and Sts. Blaise and Juliana".
Farinati's frescoes adorn the presbytery. In the apse Domenico Morone and Falconetto's frescoes

In front of the Church of Sts. Nazaro and Celso there is a Doric-Renaissance arch supported by two double columns on which a knotted piece of cloth has been sculpted around a fust. The people wanted to interpret this "cloth" as "sheets" and so, the story goes, when a young girl who was not well-off had to get married she was sent, in fun, to this church to collect, free of charge, the friars' sheets prior to the wedding!

a Benedictine cemetery. Built in the 11 C as a church for the Guests of St. John of Jerusalem, a place of recovery for the knights of the Order of Malta, it was originally dedicated to the Holy Sepulchre but when Saint Toscana's relics were brought here on 29 November, 1489 it was rededicated to her. Its appearance remained unchanged until it was bombed in 1945. Externally, the edifice is not harmonious in form, perhaps because there is no right aisle. However, a point of interest on the right is certainly the 14 C. sarcophagus and the Gothic arcosolium with fragments of frescoes. On the left, one can witness a rare phenomenon: an inscription on a Roman tombstone. Originally the church had no aisles and just a small apse but it was later enlarged, adding a side aisle on the left. The intention of doing likewise on the right was definitely there but the project was never completed. The Chapel of the Holy Sepulchre is of interest: a low-ceilinged cell where St. Toscana spent her final days on earth, nowadays, a place of popular devotion. Seven wooden Neo-Gothic statues attributed to the end of the 14 C. are kept here. Together they depict "Jesus being taken down from the Cross".

In the last bay on the left one can admire an excellent polyptych sculpted in wood, dated 1450-1500. The statues are displayed in a composite style and their grouping is heightened by paintings above while below, the central section hosts a complex "Crucifixion" whose crucifix is, in fact, older than the other sculptures. Also of interest is the 16 C "Crucifixion" (by Morone, perhaps) found in the middle between the two windows of the apse of the high altar. Liberale da Verona's triptych of "St. Toscana between Sts. Peter and

The facade of St. Toscana's Church.

John the Baptist" located on the right wall of St. Toscana's Chapel is one of this artist's most expressive masterpieces. The chapel's ceiling was painted by Domenico Tolmezzo.

Instead of taking this interesting detour, one can leave the Church of Sts. Nazaro and Celso and go down via GAETANO TREZZA (in the direction of the city centre once more) to admire the PELLEGRINI PALACE at number 56 and the RAVEGNONI PALACE next door. Then follows the CHURCH OF OUR LADY OF PARADISE 16 C. in plan but rebuilt in the 18 C. with a late 19 C. facade. It is decorated with a rich collection of relics which include the irons of St. Metrone. Among the pieces of art conserved here, the following are worthy of mention: a stational Cross and a wooden 14 C. "Crucifixion"; Liberale da Verona's "Sts. Metrone, Dominic and Anthony"; "Holy Trinity and the souls in Purgatory" by Orazio Farinati; "Madonna and Saints" by Antonio Balestra; and in the apse Paolo Farinati's "Assumption" (1565) with the majestic sepulchres of Bartolomeo dal Pozzo (1723) and Lodovico Moscardo (1681)

Almost at the end of the street, leaving behind the 14 C. ALLEGRI PALACE (actually the Police Headquarters) on the right, turn left into via San Vitale.

Continue along this street to the corner and stop at the CHURCH OF ST. PAUL IN THE FIELD OF MARS (Campo Marzio). This church was founded in the 12 C. renovated in 1285, extensively altered in the 18 C. (by Alessandro Pompei) and then practically rebuilt after World War II. It houses paintings of great value including "the Madonna, St. John the Baptist and St. Anthony of Padua presenting two gift bringers" by Paolo Veronese (C. 1565); "Our Lady with Sts. Anne, Joseph and Gioacchino with two giftbringers" by Girolamo dai Libri; "Our Lady with Sts. Peter and Paul" by Giovanni Caroto (1516); "St. Francis of Paola" by Felice Brusasorzi; "Our Lady in glory and Sts. Nicholas and Francis" by Paolo Farinati (1588) and in the sacristy, "Our Lady with Sts. Anthony Abbot and Mary Magdalen" by Francesco Bonsignori.

The GIULIARI PALACE nearby is part of the University of Verona. Walking towards the river (via San Paolo) one must stop and admire the facade of the MAROGNA PALACE which was frescoed by Giovanni and Francesco Caroto and Paolo Farinati. At the intersection, turn left into Lungadige (literally, along the

Adige) Porta Vittoria. Number 9 is the LAVEZOLA POMPEI PALACE, designed by Sanmicheli in the first half of the 14 C. and the home of the NATURAL HISTORY MUSEUM - one of the most important of its kind in Italy, renowed for its vast collection exhibited in over twenty large rooms, more specifically, for its exceptional collection of fauna (namely, fish) and Eocene flora which has come from the excavations carried out over the centuries, in the hills surrounding the village of Bolca.

At the corner of via Museo one can see the home of Paolo Veronese

(officially, Caliari) - once richly frescoed. The large building beyond the Museum, formerly the Monastery of St. Francis of Paola, has been restored recently and is these days the UNIVERSITY OF VERONA. Its Renaissance cloisters are still decorated with frescoes. One is now almost at the NEW VICTORY GATE: designed by Barbieri, it was opened by the Austrians in 1838 and erected almost beside the CHURCH OF OUR LADY OF THE OLD VICTORY - the monument Cangrande II della Scala had had built in 1350 to record his victory over Fagnano.

In 1800 Verona counted sixty mills along the Adige river in the vicinity of Victory Gate, near the Questura (police headquarters). On 6 December 1882, the millers whose existence had remained precarious since the great floods of September 1882, stopped their mills to attend a meeting at the Church of St. Mary in the Organ where, prostrated before the altar of St. Nicholas, their protector, they cried out for mercy at the hands of the river. After the ceremony they went off to a pub and enjoyed a hearty meal washed down with wine.

An unforgettable and spectacular panorama of Verona by night, taken from the top of St. Peter's hill.

BIBLIOGRAPHY

BARBETTA G., *Le mura e le fortificazioni di Verona*, ed. Vita Veronese, Verona, 1978.

BELTRAMINI G., *Le strade di Verona entro la cinta muraria*, ed. Vita Veronese, Verona, 1983.

BRUGNOLI P.P., *La Cattedrale*, ed. Vita Veronese, Verona, 1955.

BRUGNOLI P.P., *La Chiesa di San Giorgio*, ed. Vita Veronese, Verona, 1954.

CAPPELLETTI G., *La Basilica di Sant'Anastasia*, ed. Vita Veronese, Verona, 1970.

COARELLI F.-FRANZONI L., *Arena di Verona. Venti secoli di storia*, Verona, 1972.

CUMAN San-CAPORAL C., *I capitelli di Verona. Presenze vive di fede e di pietà popolare*, Vago di Lavagno (VR), 1992.

DAL POZZO B., *Le vite de' pittori, de gli scultori et architetti veronesi*, a cura di MAGAGNATO L., ed. Banca Mutua Popolare di Verona, Milano, 1967.

EDERLE G., *La Basilica di San Zeno*, ed. Vita Veronese, Verona, 1977.

FACCIOLI G., *L'Arena nella leggenda e nella storia*, Verona, 1949.

FRACAROLI B., *Verona. Guida alla città e ai suoi dintorni con consigli per il tempo libero e lo shopping e proposte di alberghi e ristoranti*, Istituto Geografico De Agostini, Novara, 1994.

LENOTTI T., *Chiese e conventi scomparsi (a destra dell'Adige)*, ed. Vita Veronese, Verona, 1955.

LENOTTI T., *Chiese e conventi scomparsi (a sinistra dell'Adige)*, ed. Vita Veronese, Verona, 1955.

LENOTTI T., *Giulietta e Romeo. Nella storia, nella leggenda e nell'arte*, Verona, 1975.

LENOTTI T., *La Bra*, ed. Vita Veronese, 1954.

LENOTTI T., *L'Arena di Verona*, ed. Vita Veronese, 1954.

LENOTTI T., *Palazzi di Verona*, ed. Vita Veronese, 1964.

MAGAGNATO L., *Arte e civiltà del Medioevo Veronese*, Roma, 1962.

MAZZI G.-MARCARINI A., *Verona e il Lago di Garda*, T.C.I., Bergamo, 1994.

PEREZ POMPEI C., *La Chiesa di San Fermo Maggiore*, ed. Vita Veronese, Verona, 1954.

RAMA G., *Proverbi de Verona. Pillole di saggezza popolare*, Verona, 1994.

REGAZZINI R. e G., *La Chiesa di Santa Maria in Organo*, ed. Vita Veronese, Verona, 1970.

S. A., *Cenni storici della Chiesa di San Eufemia. Santuario della Madonna della Salute*, Verona, 1955.

SEGALA F., Verona. La chiesa di Santa Maria Antica alle Arche scaligere. Guida storico-artistica, Verona, 1992.

SIMEONI L., *Verona. Guida storico-artistica della città e provincia*. Nuova edizione riveduta ed aggiornata a cura di ZANNONI U., ed. Vita Veronese, Verona, 1953.

STANGHELLINI L., *Guida di Verona storica ed artistica*, Verona, 1898.

TESSARI U. G., *La Chiesa di San Nazaro*, ed Vita Veronese, Verona, 1958.

TESSARI U. G., *La Chiesa di Sant'Eufemia*, ed. Vita Veronese, Verona, 1955.

TESSARI U. G., *Santa Toscana, Santa Chiara, Santa Maria del Paradiso*, ed. Vita Veronese, Verona, 1954.

TOMMASOLI A., *Pozzi e fontane di Verona*, ed. Vita Veronese, Verona, 1955.

TRECCA G., *Nuovissima guida di Verona*, Verona, 1936.

TRIDI V., *Andar per chiese a Verona*, Vago di Lavagno (VR), 1995.

INDEX OF MAIN PLACES AND MONUMENTS

Finito di stampare nel mese di agosto 1996
dalle Grafiche BUSTI S.r.l. – Vago di Lavagno (VR)
per conto della Casa Editrice DEMETRA S.r.l.

PUBS, PIZZERIAS, INNS AND RESTAURANTS

1st Itinerary

San Zeno is renowed for being the home of excellent pubs (osterie), even if many have charged their denomination to bars in recent years. Often a Veronese pub is ideal for a quick , wholsome snack - try the Bar ABAZIA, or Osteria ALLA BUSA. The Pizzeria VESUVIO is one of the very oldest pizzerias in Verona, while the Pizzeria cum Restaurant DA URBANO offers fish dishes at moderate prices.
The Restaurant cum Trattoria (Inn) AL CALMIERE combines a rich tradition with the typical Veronese cuisine.

Osteria AL BOSCAREL, Vicolo cieco Boscarello, 5 - tel. 8004574
Osteria ALLA BUSA, piazza Pozza, 19
Osteria ALL'OSTE SCURO, Vicolo San Silvestro, 10 - tel. 592650

Bar ABAZIA, Vicolo Abazia, 1 - tel. 8035847
Bar CASA VINO, vicolo Morette, 8 - tel. 8004337
Bar Osteria SAN ZENETO, Via Provolo, 6/a - tel. 590887

Pizzeria BELLA NAPOLI, Via Marconi, 16 - tel. 591143
Pizzeria VESUVIO, Via Rigaste San Zeno, 41 - tel. 595634
Pizzeria-ristorante DA URBANO, piazza Corrubio, 29 - tel. 8004254
Pizzeria-ristorante EL CANTON DE VERONA, piazzetta Santo Spirito, 3 - tel. 8003883-8032458

Trattoria DALLA IDA, Lungadige Attiraglio, 27 - tel. 8349705

Ristorante-albergo AL CASTELLO, Corso Cavour, 43 - tel. 8004403
Ristorante-trattoria AL CALMIERE, piazza San Zeno, 10 - tel. 8030765
Ristorante-trattoria ALL'ADIGE, Lungadige Catena, 35 - tel. 913376
Ristorante ANTICO TRIPOLI, Via Spagna, 2 - tel. 8035756
Ristorante NUOVO MILLEVOGLIE, Via Marconi, 72 - tel. 597517

2nd Itinerary

Along this route one passes some of the most prestigious eating places in Verona: the 12 APOSTLES, MAFFEI and ACCADEMIA. Two spots for a good, fast snack are l'Ostaria MONDO D'ORO and LE VECIETE, while pizzerias with an extensive range rival the classical trattorias (inns) which are family concerns, for example, LA MOLINARA and AL POMPIERE. Decidedly typical is the more than a century-old restaurant cum wine shop, LA BOTTEGA DEL VINO.

Ostaria A' LE PETARINE, Via San Mamaso, 6 - tel. 594453
Ostaria MONDO D'ORO, Via Mondo d'Oro, 4 - tel. 8032679
Osteria LE VECIETE, Via Pellicciai, 32 - tel. 594681

Pizzeria DA SALVATORE, Corso Porta Borsari, 39 - tel. 3030366
Pizzeria FARINA, Via Corte Farina, 4 - tel. 591032
Pizzeria PAM-PAM, Corso Porta Borsari,55 - tel. 8030363
Pizzeria-Ristorante ALLA COSTA, Via della Costa, 2 - tel. 597468-8007328
Pizzeria-Ristorante IL RITROVO, Vicolo cieco San Pietro Incarnario 5/7
  - tel. 8009494

Trattoria-Osteria SGARZERIE, Via Corte Sgarzerie, 14/a - tel. 8000312
Trattoria-Pizzeria PONTE NAVI, Via Dogana, 1 - tel. 8004517-591203
Trattoria AL BERSAGLIERE, Via Dietro Pallone, 1 - tel. 8004824
Trattoria AL POMPIERE, Vicolo Regina dell'Ungheria - tel. 8030537
Trattoria MOLINARA, Piazzetta Ottolini, 4 - tel. 595681

Ristorante ACCADEMIA, Via Scala 10 - tel. 8006072
Ristorante ALLA TORRE DEI LAMBERTI, Piazza delle Erbe, 10/b -
  tel. 8031230
Ristorante ARMANDO, Via Macello, 8 - tel. 8000892
Ristorante 12 APOSTOLI, Via Corticella San Marco, 3 - tel. 596999
Ristorante EL MOCOLETO, Via Stella, 13 - tel. 8030066
Ristorante-Enoteca BOTTEGA DEL VINO, Via Scudo di Francia, 3 -
  tel. 8004535
Ristorante-Enoteca EL CANTINON, Via San Rocchetto, 11 - tel. 595291
Ristorante GREPPIA, Vicolo Samaritana - tel. 8004577
Ristorante MAFFEI, Piazza delle Erbe, 38 - tel. 8010015
Ristorante-Pizzeria DU DE COPE, Galleria Pellicciai, 10 - tel. 595562

───────────────(**3rd Itinerary**)───────────────

This itinerary is not short of top-quality, first -class restaurants
including ALL'AQUILA, NUOVO MARCONI, ARCHE and characteristic
places such as ALLA PERGOLA, ALLA PIGNA, and the restaurant cum
trattoria (inn) DA L' AMELIA. However, this route is also lined with
moderately priced places such as the osterias (pubs): DAL DUCA,
AL CARRO ARMATO, TROTA DA LUCIANO and the nearby trattorias
FONTANINA and ALLA COLONNA.
All the pizzerias are to be recommended. Perhaps are place deserves a
speciall mention, the Osteria SOTTORIVA where we advise the visitor to
stop and enjoy the environement of a genuine old Veronese cellar with a
small carafe (quarter) of wine at an extraordinary reasonable price.

Osteria AL CARRO ARMATO, Vicolo Gatto, 2/a - tel. 8030175
Osteria DEL DUCA, Via Arche Scaligere, 2 - tel. 594474
Osteria SOTTORIVA, Via Sottoriva
Osteria TROTA DA LUCIANO, Via Trota, 3 - tel. 8004757
Osteria-Trattoria AL DUOMO, Via Duomo, 7 - tel. 8004505
Osteria-Trattoria-Enoteca PANE E VINO, Via Garibaldi, 16/a - tel. 8031548

Pizzeria SAYONARA, Piazzetta Chiavica, 5 - tel. 8031836
Pizzeria VESUVIO 3, Corso Santa Anastasia, 20 - tel. 595460
Pizzeria-Trattoria-Bar IMPERO, Piazza dei Signori, 8 - tel. 8030160

Trattoria ALLA COLONNA, Lungadige Pescheria Vecchia, 4 - tel. 566718
Trattoria ALLA PERGOLA, Piazzetta Santa Maria in Solaro, 10 - tel. 8004744
Trattoria ALLA PIGNA, Via Pigna, 4 - tel. 8004080
Trattoria FONTANINA, Via Trota, 11 - tel. 8031133
Trattoria SANTA ANASTASIA, Corso Sant'Anastasia, 27 - tel. 8009177

Ristorante -Trattoria DA L'AMELIA, Lungadige Rubele, 32 - tel. 8005526
Ristorante ALL'AQUILA, Piazza Sant'Anastasia, 4 - tel. 595044
Ristorante ARCHE, Via Arche Scaligere, 6 - tel. 8007415
Ristorante IL DESCO, Vicolo San Sebastiano, 3/5 - tel. 595358
Ristorante LA TORRETTA, Piazza Broilo, 1 - tel. 8010099
Ristorante MAZZANTI, Via Mazzanti, 6 - tel. 8010855
Ristorante NUOVO MARCONI, Via Fogge, 4 - tel. 591910-595295
Ristorante VERONA ANTICA, Via Sottoriva, 10/a - tel. 8004124

4th Itinerary

This part of Verona is characterized by numerous pizzerias, all good,
which are often certified restaurants as well. The Ristorante ALLA
FIERA DA RUGGERO is strategically placed for those going to the fair
(but there are other restaurants equally as good in the area) as is the
Trattoria DA ALDO not far from the railway station at Porta Nuova. The
TRE CORONE, TORCOLO and CIOPETA are all long-standing tradition.

Pizzeria AL DOLLARO, Corso Porta Nuova, 78/a - tel. 8032341
Pizzeria DELLE NAZIONI, Via Oriani, 2 - tel. 8033503
Pizzeria NASTRO AZZURRO, Vicolo Listone, 4 - tel. 8004457-596527
Pizzeria TORRE 5, Corso Porta Nuova - tel. 597832
Pizzeria-Trattoria ARENA, Vicolo 3 Marchetti, 1 - tel. 590503
Pizzeria-Trattoria PALLONE, Via del Pontiere, 3 - tel. 8011530

Trattoria DA ROMANO, via Valverde, 28 - tel. 8002686
Trattoria TRE MARCHETTI, Vicolo Tre Marchetti, 19/b - tel. 8030463
Trattoria VALVERDE, Via Valverde, 66 - tel. 8006791

Ristorante-Pizzeria AI DUE FORNI, Via Tezone, 2 - tel. 502045
Ristorante-Pizzeria ADRIATICO, Via Mario, 14 - tel. 8031271
Ristorante-Pizzeria AL BRACIERE, Via Adigetto, 6/a - tel. 597249-597062
Ristorante-Pizzeria IL CALICE, Via Pallone, 20 - tel. 8004892
Ristorante-Pizzeria LISTON, Via Dietro Listone, 19 - tel. 8034003
Ristorante-Pizzeria MARECHIARO, Via Sant'Antono, 15 - tel. 8004506
Ristorante-Trattoria DA ALDO, Piazzale XXV Aprile, 9 - tel. 569609
Ristorante ALLA FIERA DA RUGGERO, Via Scopoli, 9 - tel. 508808
Ristorante ARCOVOLO, Via Leoncino, 39 - tel. 8031212
Ristorante CIOPETA, Vicolo Teatro Filarmonico, 2 - tel. 8006843
Ristorante IL CENACOLO, Via Teatro Filarmonico, 10 - tel. 592288

Ristorante RUBIANI, Piazzetta Scalette Rubiani, 3 - tel. 8006830
Ristorante SCALIGERO, Via Amatore Sciesa, 27 - tel. 8030001
Ristorante TORCOLO, Via Cattaneo, 11 - tel. 8030018-8030440
Ristorante TRE CORONE, Piazza Brà, 16 - tel. 8002462
Ristorante TRE RISOTTI, Via Poloni, 15 - tel. 594408

5th Itinerary

This route, which is rather long, encompasses the left bank of the
Adige: an area which was once extremely working-class but also
where, on the magnificent hills, the city of verona was first settled. In
fact, it is on these hills that most panoramic restaurant is situated - the
RE TEODORICO on St. Petr's hill. Among little lans and other - world
streets one comes across osterias (pubs) of old repute, many of which
have, in fact, broadened thei business and become trattorias (inns),
pizzerias and, perhaps, restaurants as well. For their glorious past
LA FONTANINA and MORANDIN osterias; AL SCALIN pizzeria cum
trattoria and ALLA CANNA and ALLA RANA are to be mentioned: the
trattoria DAL ROPETON sits, romantically, at the foot of the hill.

Ostaria LA STUETA, via Redentore 4/b - tel. 8032462
Osteria AI PRETI, Interrato Acqua Morta, 27 - tel. 597675
Osteria AI TRE SANTI, Via Sant'Alessio, 48 - tel. 8340017
Osteria LA FONTANINA, Via Portichetti (ang. Via San Carlo) - tel. 913305
Osteria MORANDIN, via XX Settembre, 144 - tel. 594751

Pizzeria 2000, Via XX Settembre, 91 - tel. 8034246
Pizzeria LA GROTTINA, Interrato Acqua Morta, 38 - tel. 8030152
Pizzeria Ristorante REDENTORE, Via Redentore, 15/17 - tel. 8005932
Pizzeria-Trattoria AL SCALIN, Via San Vitale, 6 - tel. 8004330
Pizzeria-Tratoria EDEN, Via Mazza, 63 - tel. 8030419

Trattoria ALLA CANNA, Via Scrimiari, 5 - tel. 594238
Trattoria ALLA RANA, Via Corticella San Paolo, 8 - tel. 8004979
Trattoria CAPITAN TRINCHETTO, Lungadige Porta Vittoria, 35 -
   tel. 8009140
Trattoria DAL ROPETON, Via San Giovanni in Valle, 46 - tel. 8030040
Trattoria FILIPPI, Via Castel San Felice, 6 - tel. 8348619
Trattoria LA RIBOLLA, Via XX Settembre, 96 - tel. 8033975
Trattoria PERO D'ORO, Via Ponte Pignolo, 25 - tel. 594645

Ristorante LE BISTRO, Interrato Acqua Morta, 20 tel. 8004383
Ristorante LE GOURMET, Via XX Settembre, 109 - tel. 8006827
Ristorante L'INCONTRO, Via Muro Padri, 48 - tel. 590015
Ristorante RE TEODORICO, Piazzale Castel San Pietro, 1 -
   tel. 8349903-8349990